THE **MIRANDA COSGROVE**
AND *iCarly*
Spectacular!

THE **MIRANDA COSGROVE**

AND *iCarly*

Spectacular!

UNOFFICIAL & UNSTOPPABLE

LIV SPENCER

ECW Press

Published by ECW Press, 2120 Queen Street East, Suite 200, Toronto, Ontario, Canada M4E 1E2
416.694.3348 / info@ecwpress.com

LIBRARY AND ARCHIVES CANADA CATALOGUING IN PUBLICATION

Spencer, Liv
The Miranda Cosgrove and iCarly spectacular! : unofficial and unstoppable / Liv Spencer.

ISBN 978-1-55022-929-5

1. Cosgrove, Miranda, 1993- — Juvenile literature. 2. iCarly (Television program) — Juvenile literature. 3. Drake & Josh (Television program) — Juvenile literature.4. Television actors and actresses — United States — Biography — Juvenile literature. 5. Motion picture actors and actresses — United States — Biography — Juvenile literature. 6. Singers — United States — Biography — Juvenile literature. I. Title.

PN2287.C634S64 2010   J791.4302'8092   C2009-905971-1

Editor: Crissy Boylan
Photo Editor: Jennifer Knoch
Design and typesetting: Tania Craan

This book was printed in February 2010 at Shanghai Chenxi Printing, in Shanghai, China.

Special thank you to David Caron, Jennifer Knoch, and Crissy Boylan for their invaluable contributions to this book. Couldn't have done it without you. — Liv

The publication of *The Miranda Cosgrove and iCarly Spectacular!* has been generously supported by the Government of Ontario through Ontario Book Publishing Tax Credit, by the OMDC Book Fund, an initiative of the Ontario Media Development Corporation, and by the Government of Canada through the Book Publishing Industry Development Program (BPIDP). **Canada**

Front Cover Photo Copyright: Chelsea Lauren/Contributor; *Back Cover Photo Copyright:* Sue Schneider/MGP Agency
Interior Photos Copyright: Sara Jaye Weiss/startraksphoto.com: 7; Michael Simon/startraksphoto.com: 8; Sthanlee Mirador/Shooting Star 9, 103, 137; Jenny Maki/Shooting Star: 10; George Pimentel/WireImage: 11; Rena Durham/Retna Ltd.: 12, 14, 19, 27, 35, 37, 39, 47, 58, 69, 76, 86; Jason Merritt/Film Magic: 13; Michael Williams/startraksphoto.com: 15, 33, 53, 71, 100; David Strick/Redux: 16; Laura Wagner/Shooting Star: 21; AP Photo/Holly Parker: 23; Steven Defalco/Shooting Star: 25; Armando Gallo/Retna Ltd.: 29; Grayson Alexander/Retna Ltd.: 31; AP Photo/Reed Saxon: 32; Evans Ward/AP Images for Nickelodeon: 36, 73; Albert Michael/startraksphoto.com: 41, 91, 93, 104; Jen Lowery/startraksphoto.com: 42, 45, 51, 61, 81, 117, 125, 140; ML/Agency Photo: 43, 75, 94; Andy Fossum/startraksphoto.com: 48, 52, 55, 64, 67, 85, 99, 101, 108, 126; Sara De Boer/Retna Ltd.: 50, 119; Lauren Greenfield/INSTITUTE: 56, 57, 59, 65; Sue Schneider/MGP Agency: 63; Trent Warner/startraksphoto.com: 78; Scott Gries/Getty Images for Nickelodeon: 82; Stephanie Diani/The New York Times: 89; LAN/Retna Ltd.: 97; R Soria/Shooting Star: 107; Charley Gallay/WireImage: 113; RD/Dziekan/Retna Digital: 121, 133; AP Photo/Dawn Villella: 122; AP Photo/Matt Sayles: 123; Stuart Wilson/Keystone Press: 127; AP Photo/Charles Sykes: 128; Amanda Edwards/PictureGroup: 131; Albert Ferreira/startraksphoto.com: 132, 136; Walter McBride/Retna Ltd.: 134; Sipa via AP Images: 139; AP Photo/Peter Kramer: 141; Jason DeCrow/AP Images for Nickelodeon: 143.

Table of Contents

INTRODUCTION

In 5, 4, 3, 2 . . .

Ever since the launch of YouTube in 2005, anyone with an internet connection and a camera has had the chance at stardom, to be recognized in an unconventional way. Every video uploaded is a performance and an audition, a way to share spoofs, songs, and bizarre talents with the world. Internetalonians everywhere realize that they not only have the freedom to choose what to watch, but they can create that content themselves.

Visionary writer/producer Dan Schneider took notice of that do-it-yourself movement, and at the end of 2006 wrote the pilot for his newest Nickelodeon show about a girl who makes her own smash hit webcast with her two best friends. But that wasn't enough — in the spirit of online collaboration, he wanted viewers to be able to contribute as well, to help shape the show into something that reflected their zany, random, and downright strange talents. It would be a show where kids could be writers, producers, and stars; in short "the land where kids rule."

He already had a lead actress in mind for this revolutionary project. Miranda Cosgrove charmed audiences all over the world in 2003's *School of Rock*, and then transitioned from goody-two-shoes to scheming sister in the hit comedy *Drake & Josh*. She was a triple threat — she could act, sing, and dance (well, Random Dance at least) — just the dynamic performer that could headline a hot new show. *iCarly* would also bring together *Drake & Josh*'s irate usher Jerry Trainor, and two newcomers to starring roles, Jennette McCurdy and Nathan Kress.

iCarly caught on fast, and new episodes grab millions of viewers, while iCarly.com attracts millions of web surfers as well. Fans can't get enough of the show or the star at its center.

chapter 1

iMiranda

Miranda's mom, Chris, has been with her every step of the way. "It's kind of a funny relationship," says Miranda, "she's definitely my mom, but she's my best friend too. We're always making jokes and stuff and my friends say we're inseparable."

Though she seems as down to earth as the girl next door, there's no denying Miranda Cosgrove has star quality. Just as Carly Shay's natural talent was recognized by thousands of web surfers in the very first episode of *iCarly*, a talent agent recognized Miranda's sparkle at the young age of three when she was at a local restaurant, Taste of L.A., with her parents. The agent wanted the toddler to join her modeling and commercial agency, but Miranda's parents didn't jump into the decision. "My mom went

home and thought about it for a while, because she had never really thought about me getting into entertainment," related Miranda. But her parents decided to let Miranda give it a try, and thousands of fans are thankful they did.

Born on May 17, 1993, Miranda Taylor Cosgrove was raised in Los Angeles, California. She is the only child of Tom, who owns a dry cleaning business, and Chris, a stay-at-home mom. Luckily, this meant that Chris could be by Miranda's side through every step of her career.

It didn't take long for Miranda to get her first taste of success. And as it turned out, success tasted a little like Mello Yello . . . since the young actress's first gig was a commercial for the soft drink. But Miranda wasn't a pro from the get-go. "I was supposed to play with this sand castle and I accidentally knocked it over. They said I wasn't very good at taking direction," she remembers.

Miranda continued to act in commercials (including ads for McDonald's and Burger King) and model in print ads (including campaigns for Kmart and *Bon Appetit* magazine), but even with her success, she still had to learn how to face a lot of rejection. She told *People*, "I auditioned for a ton of things that I didn't get. But I never got upset about it. I thought it was fun doing the lines and going in and meeting other kids and stuff."

After several years of success with commercials, Miranda's career took an exciting new direction at age eight, when she landed

her first dramatic role as young Lana Lang on the Superman drama *Smallville*. It was a small step, but one that moved her away from appearing in magazine ads and toward gracing their covers instead.

Summer School

Miranda's big break came at age nine, when she was cast in the comedy *School of Rock* (2003). The feature film is the story of a failed musician, Dewey Finn, played by the hilarious Jack Black, who gets kicked out of his band, and, having run out of money, fakes his way into being a substitute teacher for a fifth grade class. Pretending to be "Mr. Schneebly," Dewey doesn't really care about math or history, but when he realizes his students have musical talent, he wants to teach them everything he knows. He decides the best way to get back at his old band is to start a new one and win the upcoming Battle of the Bands competition. And so the eager fifth graders become musicians and crew for the sensation that's sweeping the schoolyard — the School of Rock.

Miranda, the youngest of the film's child actors, has one of the more prominent roles, playing Summer Hathaway, the class know-it-all. Although Miranda has demonstrated her musical abilities many times since *School of Rock*, her character in it is a *terrible* singer. Often actors have to take voice lessons to improve their singing for a role, but the talented Miranda actually had to take lessons to make hers worse. Miranda recalled just after filming the movie,

"There's one scene in the movie where Summer is supposed to sing bad. I'm actually pretty good because I've been taking lessons for five years. I got to have a 45-minute lesson with [Jim O'Rourke of Sonic Youth] on how to sing bad." Since her singing was so bad it would scare away any audience, Mr. Schneebly suggests Summer be a "groupie" (a super fan), but Summer insists on more responsibility and becomes the band's manager.

Like the band in the movie, *School of Rock* was a big hit, and while Black's performance garnered most of the praise, his young supporting cast didn't go unnoticed. In his review of the film, famed critic Roger Ebert noted, "The kids aren't turned into cloying little clones, but remain stubborn, uncertain, insecure and kidlike." It's exactly the kind of praise that could define Miranda's career: she's a girl who keeps it real, even when she's playing make-believe.

As she attended the School of Rock, Miranda found she had less and less time for real school. At first she went to a regular school (Maude Price Elementary) just like any other kid. She was a pretty dedicated student, but specified, "I get pretty good grades but I'm not the bookworm type. I'm more laid back. I'll do my homework at 10 o'clock and finish it at one in the morning." Like a lot of students, one thing that could get her worked up, though, was a test. "In elementary school, I used to go crazy over tests," she remembers. "One time I asked the janitor when I'd have to take the SATs. I worried about it all year!" But as Miranda's career took off, attending regular school became more difficult, and the fifth grade was her last year there. Her parents briefly tried online school, before switching to homeschooling, which later would become on-set schooling with a tutor.

Miranda rocking the red carpet at the 2003 Toronto International Film Festival with *School of Rock* costars Rebecca Brown, Robert Tsai, Kevin Clark, and Joey Gaydos.

Homeschooling fits in with her busy life, but Miranda admits sometimes she does feel like she's missing out on the traditional school experience. "Sometimes when my friends have had an awesome day at school or they see some guy they like, I'll be like, 'Oh, I didn't get to do that,'" but she's eager to add, "I love acting so much that it outweighs the few things I don't get to do."

Miranda found big-screen success with *School of Rock*, and was also following her earlier *Smallville* appearance with other roles on television including a guest spot on *Grounded for Life* and voice work for *What's New Scooby-Doo?* These were minor parts, but then she got the opportunity to audition for a recurring character on a TV show made for kids: Nickelodeon's *Drake & Josh*. Miranda remembers this pivotal point in her career well: "I remember auditioning

Miranda studying hard on the set of *Drake & Josh*. In 2009 that work paid off when she was inducted into the National Honor Society. But ever modest, the ace student jokes, "My mom is all excited about it, but I thought it was a rip-off because all I got was a pin."

for *Drake & Josh* because it was, like, the first thing I auditioned for that I really knew about, because it was a kids' thing. That kind of got me more excited about it."

The young actress would be cast as Megan Parker, Drake's pesky and conniving younger sister who often torments the boys. Not only did her role on *Drake & Josh* get Miranda on the Nickelodeon radar, but it would also provide her with important acting experience and give an only child two "older brothers" who would be Miranda's role models for future success.

Totally Random Facts About Miranda

- Can make her eyes vibrate
- Is terrified of spiders
- Has a toy poodle, Pearl
- Her mom calls her Randy or Randall (which she hates)
- Other career goal: marine biologist
- Favorite food: cupcakes

chapter 2

Head of the Class

Creator of *Drake & Josh* and head of his own company, Schneider's Bakery, Dan Schneider has been called "arguably the most successful tween-show creator/producer of his generation" and "the master of a television genre." But his entry into show business was a fluke. While in college, Dan was stopped by a casting agent and asked to audition for a bit part in a movie. His decision to try out shaped both the rest of his life, as well as those of countless young actors, and helped make Nickelodeon the successful network it is today.

Born in Memphis, Tennessee, on January 14, 1966, Daniel J. Schneider grew up with parents Harry and Carol, and graduated White Station High School as senior class president. After taking some classes at Harvard University and at Memphis State University, Dan landed the small, but life-changing, movie role and moved to Los Angeles to pursue an acting career. He appeared in a number of films in the mid-'80s — *Making the Grade, Hot Resort*, cult classic *Better Off Dead* (with John Cusack), *The Big Picture* (with Kevin Bacon), and *Happy Together* (with Patrick Dempsey) — and one episode of *Fame*, the TV show set in a fictional performing arts high school. But it would be at another fictional school, New York's Monroe High, where Dan would gain national notice — as Dennis Blunden on ABC's *Head of the Class*, a show about an advanced placement class full of colorful characters and bright students. Dan described his character as "basically playing myself, except Dennis is sort of a more immature version of me. . . . I'm a much nicer guy!" Like his character, Dan was both smart and a computer whiz, having worked at an Apple repair shop before getting into acting. *Head of the Class* was a hit, regularly landing in the top-rated programs, and it ran from 1986 to 1991. After *Class* let out, Dan landed another series with future *Friends* star Matthew Perry, but

Home Free only lasted one season before being canceled.

At this point in his career, Dan took a little break from working in front of the camera, stepping off-screen to write and produce a sketch-comedy/variety show for Nickelodeon, helmed by Mike Tollin and Brian Robbins; Robbins had starred along-side Dan on *Head of the Class*. At first, Dan considered the show, *All That*, as a "'little side job' — something fun to do until I got my next acting role." Featuring great young talent like Kenan Thompson, Kel Mitchell, Amanda Bynes, and Nick Cannon, *All That* had recurring characters and sketches, celebrity impressions, and goofy segments

Dan almost "hambushed" on the set of *Goodburger* (starring Kel Mitchell and Kenan Thompson).

as well as hot musical guests, and it became a hit show soon after its premiere in 1994. As if one smash hit wasn't enough, Dan soon found himself working on the first of many *All That* spin-off shows, *Kenan & Kel*. Another turning point in his career came in 1996: "I was offered the lead role in a new TV pilot. . . . I had to decide if I wanted to go back to acting, or to continue writing and producing television. You can figure out which road I chose." And no doubt

Nickelodeon executives were counting their lucky stars he did.

Described by the *Washington Post* as a "one-man comic spark," Dan takes an approach to creating, writing, and producing shows for young audiences that has spawned hit after hit for Nickelodeon: *All That*, *Kenan & Kel*, *The Amanda Show*, *Drake & Josh*, *Zoey 101*, *iCarly*, and *What I Like About You* for the WB (now CW) network. He calls himself "a big kid," and uses his fun-loving, youthful perspective to relate to and instill confidence in his star performers. "My shows are about kids taking on the world," and are meant "to be entertaining, not educational."

In 1999, Dan was looking for talented young people to star alongside Amanda Bynes in a new sketch-comedy show for Nickelodeon, *The Amanda Show*, and he came across Drake Bell. In the show's second season, another cast member was added: Josh Peck. Together Drake and Josh were comedy genius, and Dan began dreaming up a sitcom for the two young actors.

Dan's Dynamos

In the Nickelodeon universe, if you catch Dan Schneider's eye and can show him you've got what it takes, he'll make sure you get a chance to make it big. Miranda is a perfect example: she proved herself on *Drake & Josh* and was rewarded with her own show. But Miranda wasn't the first, and considering Dan's newest projects, like *Victorious*, she won't be the last! Here's a quick look at the stars that Dan gave a chance to shine.

Kenan Thompson

Kenan got his start in *D2*, the Mighty Ducks sequel, before landing a regular spot on Dan's sketch comedy series *All That*. One of those sketches became a spin-off movie, *Goodburger* (1997) starring Kenan and his cohort Kel Mitchell. The pair's great chemistry also landed them their own show, Nick comedy *Kenan & Kel*, in which Kenan played the "straight man" in the dynamic duo, and earned himself a Kids' Choice Award for his work. Kenan's great instincts would lead to more comedic roles including spots on *The Steve Harvey Show*, and the title role in the feature film *Fat Albert*. Kenan really hit the big time as a cast member on *Saturday Night Live*.

Kel Mitchell

For several years Kenan and Kel were a package deal, so Kel's successes are closely tied to those of his costar. After *All That*, *Kenan & Kel*, and *Goodburger*, Kel went on do smaller acting gigs and voice work, including a three-year stint as the voice of T-Bone in the *Clifford the Big Red Dog* cartoon series. Kel also took his career in one direction his former partner didn't: he released a popular rap single "Watch Me Do My Thing" as his *Goodburger* character, Ed, and went on to record many more parodies of hit songs.

Amanda Bynes

After going to comedy camp, taking acting classes, and appearing in numerous stage productions, Amanda got her break when she appeared as a regular panelist on the Nickelodeon game show *Figure It Out*. Amanda had made it on to Dan Schneider's radar, and he cast her in what would be his first hit show — *All That*. After *All That*, Dan felt Amanda deserved a show of her own, and after an unsuccessful pilot created by the network, Dan created *The Amanda Show* to showcase her talent. "Amanda is such a rangy little actress — she's like a Dana Carvey or a little Carol Burnett," Dan told the *New York Times*. Amanda won a Kids' Choice Award three years in a row (from 2000 to 2002 for Best Television Actress), and *The Amanda Show* was one of the Nick's biggest hits. After it wrapped in 2002, Amanda kept right on working, starring in *What I Like About You* and in several movies including *Big Fat Liar* (2002), *What a Girl Wants* (2003), *She's the Man* (2006), *Hairspray* (2007), and *Easy A* (2010).

Jamie Lynn Spears

Originally best known for being the little sis of Miss Oh-My-God-That-Britney's-Shameless, Dan saw past Jamie's older sister's celebrity and figured out that star power ran in the family. After making her acting debut in Britney's feature film *Crossroads*, Jamie Lynn landed a regular role on *All That*, where she proved to viewers that she was a top-notch performer. As with Drake Bell and Josh Peck, Dan wanted Jamie Lynn to have a proper showcase for her talents and created *Zoey 101*, casting the young performer as its title character, Zoey Brooks. Fans recognized what Dan had already seen, and the show lasted four seasons (from 2005 to 2008), with Jamie Lynn taking home a Kids' Choice Award and the show earning an Emmy nomination. After *Zoey*, Jamie Lynn returned to her home state of Louisiana to raise her daughter Maddie and hopes to study business at college.

chapter 3

Drake Bell

At a very young age, Drake Bell realized that acting was a sweet deal — literally. Drake remembers, "When I was about five I did a commercial for Whirlpool sitting on a tree stump eating a popsicle that dripped all over my clothes. After that, I was like, 'You know what? I think I'll just stick with this!'"

Jared Drake Bell was born on June 27, 1986, in Orange County, California, the third son of Robin Dodson, a professional billiards player, and Joe Bell. After his appearances in ads, Drake soon landed other acting jobs, including a guest spot on *Home Improvement* and a chance to save the world in the 1995 sci-fi flick *Drifting School*. He also played young David in the 1995 adaptation of Terrence Davies' novel *The Neon Bible*. But Drake's first participation in a major feature film was as Jesse Remo, the son of an injured sports star, in Tom Cruise's 1996 smash hit *Jerry Maguire*. After that, Drake was cast in more popular TV sitcoms including *Seinfeld*, *The Drew Carey Show*, and *Caroline in the City*. The young actor also secured parts in two TV movies, *Dragonworld: The Legend Continues* (1999) and *Chasing Destiny* (2001), as well as the 2001 feature film *High Fidelity*.

But it was *The Amanda Show* that would really make Drake Bell a household name. From 1999 to 2001, Drake was featured as a regular performer in the sketch comedy and variety series, and also recorded the show's theme song. It was here he befriended future partner-in-crime Josh Peck, and they impressed Nickelodeon's producers so much that they would soon be starring in a show of their own.

In 2004, Drake began working on *Drake & Josh*, playing Drake Parker, the super cool ladies man, who his costar Josh calls "debonair with charisma." Drake is far less responsible than his stepbrother Josh, and often gets the duo into trouble. Although there are certainly some similarities between the musical (and girl-friendly) Drake Parker and the real-life Drake Bell, the actor admits, "I don't think I'm as cool as I am on the show." Television audiences thought he was pretty cool though, and Drake won a Kids' Choice Award for Favorite TV Actor three years in a row. After four years working on the show, Drake said, "Ending it is bitter-sweet. It's like graduating high school. You miss all your friends, but now I can do my music more and other stuff." As it turns out, the end of the TV series wasn't the last we'd get to see of Drake and Josh, given that the boys resumed their characters for three Nickelodeon specials: *Drake & Josh Go to Hollywood* (2006), *Drake & Josh: Really Big Shrimp* (2007), and *Merry Christmas, Drake & Josh* (2008). In 2005, the Nick star could also be seen in the movie theater, playing one of Rene Russo's sons in the family-friendly comedy *Yours, Mine & Ours*.

But just as everything was going Drake's way, things took a dangerous turn. On December 22, 2005, while he was waiting to make a left-hand turn at a red light, a truck collided head-on with his car. Although he was lucky enough to avoid life-threatening

Disney's *Max Keeble's Big Move* (2001), and playing a small role, "Fat Boy," in an indie flick, *Spun*. Both films made fun of Josh's weight, although Josh would focus on his nutrition and fitness and go on to lose around 100 pounds over the next five years, which opened up new kinds of roles to him.

But his weight may have added to the goofball image that helped land him a starring role on the newest television creation of *Amanda Show* producer Dan Schneider, a sitcom about two mismatched stepbrothers, *Drake & Josh*. While Drake got to be the suave, reckless, cool kid, Josh is the complete opposite — the kind of smart, responsible kid that's more popular with his parents than his classmates. But how much is Josh Peck like his fictional alias Josh Nichols? "I'm a lot like my character, though I'd like to think I'm not as dorky," Josh told the *New York Times*. "I like to do things that aren't exactly the stereotypically cool thing — play chess, go to the movies a lot. I do play a really mean air guitar." Nevertheless, Josh is fond of his character and likes being the show's funnyman. "I've always liked being the physical one — my character is sometimes the butt of jokes and sometimes he makes the jokes. In life, I'd much rather have people laughing at me than booing me. I'm cool with it. To me, there's nothing greater than making people laugh," related Josh. Josh's onscreen persona was so successful, *Drake & Josh* continued for four seasons and three spin-off movies, and won two Kids' Choice awards for Best TV Show.

Even though audiences loved Josh as the adorable funny guy on *Drake & Josh*, the young actor knew he had more to offer. He did a complete 180 by playing the school bully, George, in the 2004 indie film *Mean Creek*. George was a complicated character, and Josh had to make the bully both threatening and vulnerable. "I knew that George had to jump from one end of the spectrum to the other end," said Josh. "He had to be

Totally Random Facts About Josh

- Acting influences: Richard Pryor and Bill Cosby
- Fave actor is Ben Kingsley (his *Wackness* costar)
- Has worn an earring in his left ear since he was 12

this really good guy, sort of vulnerable and needy for this friendship, [who] really wanted to show his true self to these people. But in a second, he could throw this defense up that was just really horrible and antagonizing and mean." Despite the complexity of this role, the film's writer/director Jacob Aaron Estes had complete faith in Josh. Estes told *USA Today*, "Josh came in and blew my mind. He has a warm face, but I knew he could also be threatening." The director made the right call in casting Josh, who went on to win an Independent Spirit Award for his performance.

Josh wasn't done wowing audiences with his dramatic range, and in 2006 he provided the voice for Eddie, the opossum, in the animated feature film *Ice Age: The Meltdown*. The voice-over experience gave Josh the chance to act like a kid again: "When I was alone doing the dialogue, I got to rediscover parts of my brain that had gone dormant over the years. I rediscovered the fact that when I was seven, eight, and nine years old I had a vivid imagination. During those years I would be in my room building forts and doing character voices in my head and talking to myself. So when I was in the recording booth I would do that and create my own little world, so that I really felt I was in the Ice Age. I asked them to crank up the air conditioning so I felt genuinely cold and then I would blast off. When I was working with Seann [William Scott] who plays Crash, it was like having a hurricane and a tornado in the same room

Josh has undergone a radical transformation, losing almost 100 pounds, which he says "was about being happy in my own skin and having a healthier outlook on life," though he does joke that the weight loss opened up "parts that are of a broader range."

and we would bounce off the walls going nuts. We got on so well, it was a blast."

Having proven himself more than just another tween-TV sensation by demonstrating his tremendous range, Josh landed a starring role in the 2008 coming-of-age feature film *The Wackness*. It was another major departure for Josh, who plays a drug dealer opposite Oscar-winning actor Sir Ben Kingsley. Josh described *The Wackness* as "the first movie I've done that has totally engrossed me." And his effort paid off, with writer/director Jonathan Levine commenting, "He felt so real. So authentic. And I felt for him so much when I was looking through the camera." Josh acknowledges that this new kind of role will be a huge change for his Nickelodeon fan base. "I think *Drake & Josh* is something that spoke to me when I was 15, and now I'm 21. My tastes have matured. It was never really a conscious decision. I'm forever in debt to Nickelodeon. It made me who I am today. . . . It is a leap of faith, though, that I'm taking in my audience, and I hope they take with [it] with me."

Josh can also been seen revisiting the role of a bully in the 2008 comedy *Drillbit Taylor*, and in the drama *American Primitive* released the same year. In 2009, he was seen in *What Goes Up*, *Ice Age: Dawn of the Dinosaurs*, and the sci-fi family film *Aliens in the Attic*. Although Josh's career continues to pick up speed, the young actor remains down to earth. He told the Associated Press, "When I look in the mirror, I still see a goofball."

chapter 5

Drake & Josh

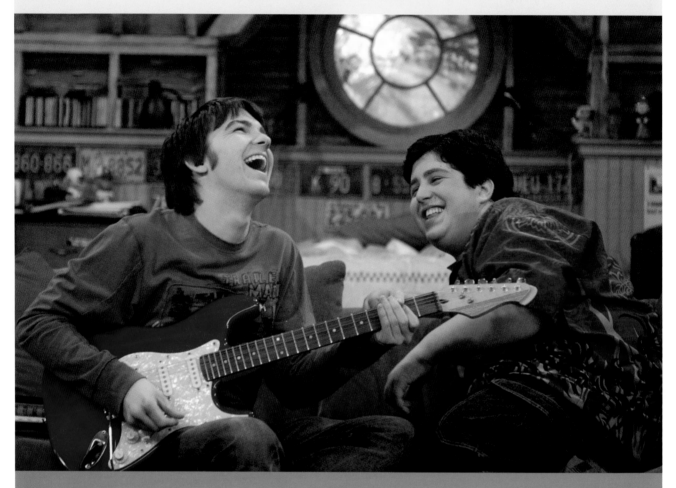

Hanging on to good times: Dan kept the couch that was the scene for many on-set laughs such as these. It now resides in his living room!

"I was definitely nervous, but all I cared about was meeting Drake and Josh," said Miranda, looking back on the days before she started working on *Drake & Josh* in the role of troublemaker Megan Parker. Miranda knew who the boys were just like the rest of her friends: from watching them on *The Amanda Show*. But now she got to work with them!

The first episode of *Drake & Josh* aired on January 11, 2004, a show about a blended family, the Parker-Nichols — Audrey Parker (played by Nancy Sullivan, who was also on *The Amanda Show*), her son Drake, daughter Megan, now living with Walter Nichols and his son Josh. At the heart of the show are Drake and Josh, two guys who go to the same high school but run in *very* different

Miranda and her two brothers all grown up at the premiere of *Merry Christmas, Drake & Josh*, which filmed two years after the last episode was taped. "It was really great to come back," Josh told MTV. "We missed each other."

crowds until they're forced together by their parents' marriage. The now-stepbrothers have to share a bedroom and end up sharing — over the course of four seasons and three TV movies — adventures, mishaps, misunderstandings, and more than their fair share of pranking by evil little Megan. Audiences loved *Drake & Josh*; its ratings were great; and the show and its cast won Kids' Choice Awards again and again.

Even though onscreen Drake and Josh can't stand pesky Megan, real-life Drake and Josh love Miranda like a little sister — showing her the ropes of Nick fame, pulling friendly on-set pranks, going to the movies together, and keeping in touch long after the series ended. As the final season wrapped filming, working alongside her famous costars no longer gave Miranda any trace of the nerves she once had: "It's just been so much fun getting to work with Drake and Josh. I mean, they're like two of the funniest guys ever, and they make me laugh every day a million times. [When I first started *Drake & Josh*] I was like, oh my god. But now it's really comfortable, and it's really fun." As Miranda became old enough to start dating, Josh said, "I'm ridiculously protective — I don't think anyone is good enough for her." For Miranda, *Drake & Josh* was her first regular job on a TV series, and she was devastated when it ended. Not because she was out of a gig, but because she had made lifelong friendships and was sad to see an era come to an end. "When we finished *Drake & Josh* I was totally upset. It was hard knowing I wasn't going to be with those people every day."

For Dan Schneider, *Drake & Josh* had the perfect run, as he explained on his DanWarp.com blog. "We'd done the show for a long time. Drake had worked with me at Nickelodeon for seven years. Josh six. . . . By season 4 of *Drake & Josh*, the boys were around 19 years old, and the network already had 60 episodes. . . . I'm happy that *Drake & Josh* went out at its PEAK of popularity. The final two-parter [*Really Big Shrimp*] got our highest rating ever. So, *Drake & Josh* was never really canceled. We all just agreed the time had come to move on. It was really sad to say goodbye to that show."

Never one to rest (no, really, he *never* rests), Dan began cooking up a new show as *Drake & Josh* was in its final season and he knew just who would be at the center of it. He'd pulled supporting cast members from all his previous shows to star in his next one, and he wasn't about to switch up his winning formula. Explained Dan, "*All That* begat *The Amanda Show* begat *Drake & Josh* begat *iCarly*. It's become my method." Miranda Cosgrove would star in his next project, an actress he described as "very mature and sophisticated in some ways. And she's very little girl in other ways, and I just love that about her." Fans of *Drake & Josh* had loved her as Megan Parker, and it was time to find out if that admiration would translate to her next, and much bigger, role as Carly Shay.

iCarly
DIY TV

chapter 6

Miranda's always compared to Miley, but she's got nothing but respect for the dynamite performer — in fact she's a big fan! And Miley's a fan of Miranda too — she tweeted "laying around watching iCarly!!! :)"

As *Drake & Josh* was winding down in November 2006, Dan Schneider was already hard at work on an idea for a new show. He wanted it to be about an ordinary girl who got an extraordinary opportunity: the chance to act on her favorite television show. Dan wrote the pilot, calling the show *Starstruck*, and it got an enthusiastic reaction from the Nickelodeon execs.

But sitting at home with his wife Lisa Lillien (the creator of the *Hungry Girl* books and web phenomenon) and a friend, Dan realized there was a way to make the show more realistic and original: the main char-

acter wouldn't star in a TV show, she would make her own web show. He threw out *Starstruck*, and started again. He had a new pilot in December, and with Nickelodeon's quick approval, they started shooting in January 2007.

While Dan's *Starstruck* may have hit the recycling bin, many fans have noted the similarities between *Starstruck* and Disney's *Sonny with a Chance*, which premiered in February 2009, starring one of the Mouse House's rising stars, Demi Lovato. It's not known whether there's any definite connection between Dan's abandoned pilot and the new Disney hit. Dan attests that "everyone in the entertainment business knows what everyone else is doing," though he shrugs off the similarities between the two shows with good humor and the old adage, "Imitation is the sincerest form of flattery."

But before *Sonny with a Chance*, *iCarly* was being compared to another hit Disney show: *Hannah Montana*. Nickelodeon president Cyma Zarghami admitted that the show about the wigged wonder with the double-identity is a big hit, but added, "Kids probably look at it and say, 'That can't happen.' I think *iCarly* is a little more realistic to what could happen, though still with fantastical appeal."

If kids were going to live out their fantasies on *iCarly*, Dan wanted to use everyday actions and events, and his focus was on the biggest daydream out there: triumphing over adults. Dan wanted to have a show where young people could be their own goofy selves at full volume. He explains, "When you're a kid, most of the time you're being told to shut up by adults. In school: be quiet. Your dad's watching a show: be quiet. Even the kids who seem to have a lot of freedom, their lives are pretty controlled. So what I try to do on my show is to have kids come out on top. They're the smartest ones in the room. They're the ones in charge."

Dan also knew what he *didn't* want — sappy scenes where lessons are learned and everything comes together, which are often a big part of television aimed at the younger set. (Dan even spoofs those schmaltzy happily-ever-after movies on the *iCarly* website; check out *Kelly Cooper: Terrible Movie* for a perfect example.) About his show, he says, "There's no resolution and I love that. And let me tell you, it took me a long time to win those battles [with the network]. The sweet

wrap-up scenes? Who wants to see 'em? Let's just end on big funny."

After having worked with Dan on two shows, Miranda can sum up what makes her producer's shows such a success: "He knows what kids like. It's really difficult — it's harder than people think: to make kids laugh but not insult them. He's really good at that."

With all these basic principles, it really comes down to one thing: Dan trusts his instincts and asks himself, "When I was a kid, would I have wanted to watch this?"

But what's a great script without a star? Luckily, Dan had just the person in mind. He'd already worked with Miranda on *Drake & Josh*, and had her in mind for the starring role of Carly Shay. Miranda had the comic chops and the perfect girl-next-door vibe. He knew Miranda was just the right fit for his title character: "She's just a girl. She's beautiful and cool, and she could also be your best friend." Helping to cast Miranda, talent executive Paula Kaplan knew that Dan's choice was a good one: "There aren't a lot of actresses who are beautiful and can get a laugh. Everyone is really drawn to her."

But beyond her looks and abilities, Dan knew that Miranda was a great person to work with. Having gotten to know her on the set of *Drake & Josh*, *iCarly*'s creator has nothing but praise for Miranda: "She's a star. She is one of the classiest little girls that I've ever met. I don't believe I've ever heard her complain about anything, I don't think I've ever seen her in a bad mood once in my life."

And what did the young actress think of Schneider creating a show for her? "I was freaking out when I heard Dan would make a show for me," she said. "I was in shock."

But after the initial shock wore off, Miranda felt extremely comfortable in the role. "It's just about a girl who is like a normal teenager going through life," she explains. "She's dealing with boys, friends, and all the same things normal teenagers are dealing with, but she also has a super popular web show, and she's kind of underground famous."

iCarly may sometimes focus on crazy stunts and weird talents, but the characters also deal with everyday issues. Miranda reflects, "A lot of the skits have happened to me — so it's even easier to act it out if you've been through it." Hopefully she's not talking about parachuting out of a rusty plane over Japan or getting in the ring with a champion mixed martial arts fighter. But you never know.

Miranda also found becoming Carly Shay an easy transition because the two have more in common than their appearance. "I'm a little like her," says Miranda. "I mean, I'm really into, like, my family and friends and stuff, but then also she always has a plan for everything, and she's really good with that. But when things go wrong in my life, I usually go crazy and I have a friend that comes up with a plan."

With *iCarly*, creator Dan Schneider was the man with a plan and brought together other top Nick talent for Miranda's sup-

Hi-larious and always unpredictable: the cast gets as excited as viewers for the new *iCarly* episodes!

porting cast. "Dan has a really magical touch," said the green slime network's prez, Cyma Zarghami. "He's got a knack for identifying great talent. I think he learned a lot from his own experiences."

Jennette McCurdy caught Schneider's eye when she did a guest spot on *Zoey 101*, and he he wrote the role of Sam Puckett, Carly's gutsy, loud-mouth best friend, especially for her. Rounding out this tremendous teen trio was Nathan Kress, who'd been cast in a Freddie-like bit part on *Drake & Josh*. And when it came to cast the token adult, Carly's older brother and guardian, Miranda had a familiar cast mate in Jerry "Crazy Steve" Trainor, who she'd just finished working with on *Drake & Josh*.

In an unusual vote of confidence, Nickelodeon ordered 13 episodes of *iCarly* without a finalized cast, a pilot episode, or a title. They had faith in Dan Schneider's judgment, and in turn, Dan had faith in his show. "From the beginning, I was pretty sure *iCarly* was going to be popular. I've made lots of shows, for a long time, and I learn more with every one. But what made me feel extra confident about *iCarly* was THE CAST — all four of them are so good and funny," wrote Dan.

Test audiences agreed. When the pilot was shown to four groups of 8- to 11-year-olds in Teaneck, New Jersey, 27 of 32 kids gave the show an A or an A+. The *iCarly* crew had only been haunting the halls of Ridgeway Junior High School for a week, but they'd already been given a passing grade.

Jennette McCurdy

chapter 7

Although Jennette McCurdy's successful career is evidence that she was born under a lucky star, her inspiration to enter show business came from near tragedy. When she was only two years old, her mother was diagnosed with breast cancer and confined to the hospital for months at a time. Jennette and her three older brothers spent a lot of time there keeping their mother company, and tried to keep their minds off things by watching the original *Star Wars* trilogy over and over again. Jennette recounted, "A motto that we lived by was 'The Force is with mommy; she can do this; she'll be OK; the Force is with her.'" The Force may have factored in her mother's miraculous recovery, which was a lasting inspiration to Jennette in two ways. First, it showed her what people can overcome despite the odds, and second, it introduced her to Harrison Ford's Han Solo, who made her want to be an actor.

At first, her family tried to dissuade her, because unlike her *iCarly* character, Sam Puckett, Jennette was extremely shy. She remembers, "I was so shy you won't find any pictures of my face, just the back my head, because I always turned my head when a camera was around." But she wouldn't let her shyness stand between her and her dream, and she continued to try to convince her family until her mom helped her find an agent.

Born June 26, 1992, in Garden Grove, California, Jennette Michelle Faye McCurdy was only seven when she got her first job,

Jennette was inspired to take up skating by the 2006 Winter Olympics, and started skating under the close eye of her coach Igor in 2007. Check out her on-ice moves on her YouTube channel!

one that would not only spark her acting career, but her music career as well. "I was seven and I did an open casting call for Faith Hill's 'The Way You Love Me' music video, where I played her daughter. I loved the song and just got really interested in

Jennette at the Revlon Run/Walk for Women with her mom, who has been an inspiration to the actress her whole life. She wrote to her mom on her website: "You give me energy, hope, excitement, and drive. I'm so grateful for that!"

country music from that moment on," she told *People*. At age eight she hit another career milestone with her first television appearance when she was cast in an episode of *MADtv*. Despite this comedic beginning, Jennette's next roles were more serious: guest spots on TV dramas such as *CSI*, *Law & Order: Special Victims Unit*, *Medium*, and *Judging Amy*.

Jennette continued her streak of serious roles with a part in the 2003 action flick *Hollywood Homicide*. Although it was a small part, it was one of tremendous importance for the young actress. Not only was it her feature film debut, but it also gave her a chance to work with her inspiration: Harrison Ford.

Over the next couple of years Jennette continued with small roles in television series like *Malcolm in the Middle* and *Will & Grace*, but it was her guest appearance on *Zoey 101* that would capture the attention of Nickelodeon and Dan Schneider. Jennette played Trisha Kirby, Dustin's new girlfriend, in the season 2 episode "Bad Girl."

iCarly was Jennette's first gig as a cast member on a show, playing Sam Puckett, Carly's cohost and BFF. She was ecstatic when she found out, celebrating with tears, screams, and handstands. Dan Schneider, who created the role of Sam with her in mind, has nothing but praise for the young starlet. The producer calls her "a natural talent," and describes how different Jennette is from Sam: "I love actors who are nothing like their character. Sam is rude. Sam is brazen. She's a scofflaw and a little bit mean. And then you yell, 'Cut!' and Jennette is this sweet little girl who couldn't be nicer. It's pretty cool to see."

Totally Random Facts About Jennette

- Favorite food: grilled cheese
- Celeb crushes:
  Gavin DeGraw, Johnny Depp, Jesse McCartney
- Wears mismatched socks every day
- Favorite colors: pink and purple
- Fave person to hang out with: her mom

Jennette also recognizes that there are a couple of major differences between her and her character: "I just don't like pushing people down and slamming them into lockers and eating bacon all the time!" And maybe this difference is part of the reason Jennette has a blast playing Sam, who the actress admires "because she's really smart, she thinks on the ball, and she has some great ideas. She's feisty and wacky and zany and a great character to play. She's so much fun." It seems all of the *iCarly* actors have slipped comfortably into their characters. "I think we were all really fortunate in that we were able to get right into our characters," she observes. "We got it, and we were able to have great chemistry."

Reviewers were quick to recognize Jennette's comedic talents as one of the highlights of the show. The *Washington Post* praised, "As sassy, uninhibited Sam, McCurdy is already adept at slapstick and physical comedy."

As if being on a hit TV show and trying to keep up with school (she is home-schooled by her mom and a teacher on set) wasn't enough to handle, Jennette also revealed another side of herself when she went to work on an album in 2008. The young songstress wasn't content just to provide the vocals either; she took lessons in guitar and drums and was involved in song-writing as well. Jennette shared some of the process of writing her single "So Close" with Popstar.com: "I find that writing a song is kind of like spilling your soul. The song started with a personal experience of mine and I told my cowriters Ty and Joy that I really wanted to write about this because it was something I felt strongly about. So we sat around and we all talked and talked and talked about the situation and we all typed on our laptops until we have a total of 11 pages of typed words. We had to sift through those and find stuff that would work lyrically for a song and then we all worked on the melody. It was a long process but a lot of fun."

Lyrically, "So Close" is about what it's like to have a crush on someone who feels close, but remains distant. Jennette told JustJaredJr., "It's a song that I find really close to my heart, and I really hope that [people] find it close to their heart, because I think everybody can find a story in this song." Musically, it has "a pop country feel with a rock beat in the background." The single was released on March 10, 2009, reaching 16 on the iTunes Country chart and 53 on the iTunes Pop Chart. Jennette followed this release with another single, a cover of Amanda Stott's "Homeless Heart," which reached 43 on the iTunes Country charts.

Always eager to connect with her fans, Jennette cleverly found another way to share her talent: YouTube. News of her videos spread like wildfire and on June 27, 2009, when the singer uploaded an informal video of her in her hotel bathroom, singing the Mötley Crüe tune "Home Sweet Home" (also covered by Carrie Underwood), it got a quarter of a million hits in one day, and

the next day she was the number one most watched musician on YouTube. Jennette's YouTube channel also features videos of her singing "Right as Rain" by Adele, "What Hurts the Most" by Rascal Flatts, Carole King's "So Far Away" and "You've Got a Friend." (Jennette's accompanied on guitar by her producer, Ty, on the last two.) With stellar performances such as these, Jennette's attracted over 140,000 subscribers and is number 26 on YouTube's list of most subscribed musicians.

With her talent and popularity, the music industry couldn't overlook her for long, and on July 6, 2009, Jennette announced on her website that she signed with Capitol Records Nashville. She wrote, "I am honored, ecstatic, elated, and overwhelmed with joy! Capitol's expertise in country music will allow me the opportunity to give you guys the best I have to give in songwriting, singing, and performing. For those of you waiting for my album, this fantastic news will present a slight delay in that release — but I promise you, I will give you everything I have to make this album something you love and remember. I will now be able to take you all along on this wonderful ride and I hope you enjoy seeing the step-by-step process of the making of my record."

After the extended second season of *iCarly* wrapped, Jennette (accompanied, as usual, by her mom) headed off to Nashville to start working on her record. Despite the break from her rigorous filming schedule, her time in the legendary city of music wasn't a vacation. "I've been working on my album non-stop!" she wrote. "I still can't believe that I am walking into rooms and writing songs with songwriters that I admire and look up to so much. It's just crazy. I've worked with dozens of writers and they have all been such wonderful, warm, and welcoming people. I've also listened to tons of 'outside' songs, which means they come from writers whose publishers would like to pitch the songs to me. So basically, between songs that I've cowritten and outside songs, I'm hearing songs all day long. I'm actually having a hard time falling asleep at night because songs won't stop running through my brain."

With her music climbing the charts and *iCarly* climbing the ratings, what's next for Jennette? She'll keep writing (she's written four screenplays, several episodes of a TV series, poems, short stories, a book, and writes a monthly 32-page magazine called "Original Girl" for girls eight and up), not to mention she has her eye on the director's chair. But it seems this rising star isn't keen on downtime anyway: "After five days of hard work on *iCarly*, on the weekend I think, 'Gosh, I'm bored!'"

chapter 8

Nathan Kress

Like his *iCarly* costar Jennette McCurdy, Nathan Karl Kress knew that he wanted to act at a very young age. He remembers, "Since I was very young, probably two or three, I had really good memorization skills. I would memorize stuff from TV and perform it for my family. I was the little performer for most of my early life. So eventually my mom caught on that I might want to get into acting."

Born on November 18, 1992, in Glendale, California, Nathan has two older brothers, Andrew and Kevin, who also caught the acting bug, but have made it a hobby and not a career. Nathan, on the other hand, jumped right into being a professional and burned out after a few intense years of auditions, casting calls, and some work (most notably voice work for *Babe: Pig in the City*). He ended up retiring from show business at age six, long before most kids have even considered their career choices!

But when the former pro took the stage for his school performance of *The Emperor's New Clothes*, he remembered what he loved about acting, and decided to actively look for work once again.

Nathan started his return to showbiz on familiar ground, providing voices for the 2005 computer-animated feature film *Chicken Little*. The same year he also landed a guest appearance on *House* and did a five-episode stint as a sketch character on *Jimmy Kimmel Live*. Nathan would follow up this success with guest spots on such popular shows as *Without a Trace* and *The Suite Life of Zack & Cody*, but it would be his six-line spot on Nickelodeon's *Drake & Josh* that would be his biggest break.

Drake & Josh producers noticed how well he handled the character, which was a sort of prototype for his Freddie character on *iCarly*. In a scene cut from the episode, Nathan's character hits on Miranda's and she keeps turning him down. When Nathan was called back to audition a year later for Freddie, he got the part. "I was really excited because this would be the second time I'd get to work with Dan Schneider. I had this really small part on *Drake & Josh* that was an absolute blast to work on."

Nathan's new role would be as Fredward "Freddie" Benson, the tech-wiz on *iCarly*, who takes care of the behind-the-scenes production while Carly and Sam perform. He has a huge crush on Carly, while he and Sam enjoy an insult-and-prank-filled love/hate relationship. With Nathan playing the role,

> ## Totally Random Facts About Nathan
> - Loves the *Lord of the Rings* movies
> - Has an annual pass to Disneyland
> - Favorite color: green
> - Favorite ice cream flavor: banana fudge ripple

geeks are cooler than ever and *Variety* noted, "Nerdy Freddie gives A.V. club enthusiasts a much needed image boost."

The role was a comfortable fit, and Nathan admits there are some similarities between him and his character: "We're both definitely into the whole tech thing, but he's a much bigger geek about it than I am. One of the other big things is that he is really devoted to his friends, when he says he is going to do something he does it, and he really cares about the people he is with."

The year after he was cast as Freddie, Nathan landed another job with his home network: a starring role in the 2008 Nickelodeon original film *Gym Teacher: The Movie*. Nathan played Rolland Waffle, the klutzy transfer student, who an ambitious PE teacher tries to make into a star athlete. "*Gym Teacher: The Movie* truly has something for everyone in the family," announced Marjorie Cohn, an executive at Nickelodeon, who called it "a funny yet

climbing, the jumping, and sit-ups and push-ups and all that. . . . I definitely wasn't a bum before I started, but by the time I got back I had some really sore muscles that I didn't know I had before." Nathan got to attend an unusual premiere for *Gym Teacher*: on a ship! The flick premiered on board the Nickelodeon cruise, with Nathan in attendance to get reactions from his fans first hand.

Nathan's happy with the way his career is going and says, "I wouldn't trade my life with anybody else's right now," but after having already left acting behind once, he's also considering other options. "I do hope to be an adult actor. But if it doesn't work out, I've been thinking about doing something in the medical therapy field, chiropractics or something like that. I've always been into the idea of helping people medically."

touching story of redemption, for all those who like to root for the underdog."

Though the role was still in Nathan's comedic comfort zone, it challenged him in new ways. He related, "It was actually very physical and I had to really get in the part. I had to do all the training, the running, the

Jerry Trainor

Gerald William Trainor was born on January 21, 1977, in San Diego, California, and he fell in love with acting while he was still in grade school, after playing a part in a *Hansel and Gretel* spoof. In his teens, Jerry performed in plays at University of San Diego High School where his mother is a math teacher. "My parents are just super cool. They were like, 'Whatever you want to do, whatever you're good at, do it to the best of your ability and we're going to sup-

port you.'" His older sister, Liz, also got into showbiz, working on the other side of the camera as a script supervisor. At the age of 22, Jerry got his first television role on MTV's *Undressed*, before being cast in the 2001 sci-fi/horror film *Donnie Darko*. Jerry later appeared in popular television shows such as *Malcolm in the Middle*, *Boston Public*, *My Wife and Kids*, *ER*, and *Angel*, and scored a small role in 2004's cheerleader flick sequel *Bring It On Again*. After all of these smaller roles, Jerry got a break when he was cast in a recurring role as Brian the A.V. guy on *Crossing Jordan*. Since these guest roles weren't enough to consistently pay the bills, Jerry was sometimes working two or three jobs just to make ends meet.

But Jerry really made his mark when he was cast as Crazy Steve on *Drake & Josh*. Crazy Steve works at the same movie theater as Josh, and got his nickname because of his uncontrollable tantrums. "The comedy in Crazy Steve is the switch," Jerry told the *Orange County Register*. "He's totally like a normal guy, you see him and he's this pleasant little usher, and the minute you say anything sideways, the switch goes off and he explodes." Viewers loved this goofy character, and Nickelodeon knew they had found a good thing. Dan Schneider admits that Jerry "takes a funny line in the script and makes it 10 TIMES FUNNIER. Always. I think Jerry could easily end up being a huge movie star in hilarious movies."

When *Drake & Josh* wrapped, Jerry had

to go back to his day job in the audience services department for Los Angeles's Center Theater Group, which was "heart-wrenching." But Dan hadn't forgotten him and wanted to give him a chance at the role of Spencer. Jerry remembers, "I got an email from Dan directly. It was like, 'So it's Miranda's show, there's a big-brother role, whaddya think?' And I thought, 'Do you know where I *am* right now?'"

The email was Jerry's ticket out of the ticket office, and he landed the role of Spencer Shay, Carly's older brother. Jennette says she knew that Jerry was the perfect fit for the big-kid older bro: "I went in with Miranda to read with five Freddies and three Spencers who were going for the part. As soon as I met Jerry, I thought he *had* to be Spencer."

Spencer's a sculptor who is a good guardian to Carly, despite his frequent mishaps like short-circuiting the apartment or accidentally ending up on a bus to Canada. Though Spencer seems too crazy to be real, Jerry doesn't think he's completely different from his character. He told *Nick Magazine*, "We are both pretty optimistic and energetic and a little off the wall, but he's much more wacky-crazy, and I'm a little more grounded."

Playing Spencer, Jerry gets to be wacky-crazy and weird, often making the other actors crack up on set. Drawing out the similarities between the actor and the character, Dan Schneider wrote, "Both Jerry and Spencer are FUN to be around. Funny, silly,

a bit crazy, warm, friendly, and extremely nice." Audiences agree: *Variety* called Jerry-as-Spencer "endearingly goofy," the *Washington Post* compared the "physically gifted" comic actor to Jim Carrey, and he was nominated for a 2009 Teen Choice Award for Choice TV Actor–Comedy. While he's still at work on the Nickelodeon show, Jerry could also be spotted on the big screen in *Waking Dreams* (2007) and *Pieces of Dolores* (2008).

Some actors would look down on working on a show for kids starring kids, but Jerry doesn't see it as anything but the success he was seeking for so long: "To finally be working every day as an actor — and not only that, as a funny part on a funny show that tons of kids watch? It's literally a dream come true."

Totally Random Facts About Jerry

- His dog, Shoe, is half Jindo
- Has around 30,000 songs in his iTunes
- Favorite bands: Tokyo Police Club and Radiohead
- Loves *Arrested Development*

Life on Set

chapter 10

words that are going to be spoken by the actors." That's not to say that being a writer is a walk in the park; from start to finish an episode takes about 40 hours of writing and revising, and after one late-night writing session, Dan tweeted at 3 a.m.: "Steve and I just finished another *iCarly* one-hour special script. Whew! Table read in six hours. Wow. ZZZZZZZZZZZZZ . . ."

Cut to: Monday morning, Nickelodeon on Sunset, an old theater from the 1930s, where *All That, Kenan & Kel, Drake & Josh*, and *The Amanda Show* were all filmed. The cast assembles there for a "table read," where the actors sit around a table and read the script out loud for the writers, director, and producers. Based on that read-through, the writers may make some cuts and changes. Often the scripts are too long — sometimes up to six minutes (or roughly six pages) have to be cut to hit an episode's 23-minute length. In the afternoon, the actors will do light rehearsals, getting more familiar with the episode.

On Tuesday and Wednesday, the actors rehearse all day, then perform a run-through on Wednesday afternoon. When the actors bring their own personalities and perspective to the characters, sometimes the writers will be inspired to change the script. "When I come to see the run-throughs, I'm sometimes surprised by something the actors and director have come up with on their own, during rehearsal, and sometimes it's awesome and I use it in the show," explains Dan. "Jerry Trainor, for example,

The characters were cast, and it was time to get down to work. But where do you even begin making a show like *iCarly*? It starts with Dan Schneider and his team, who first have to write a script for the episode. Despite having to produce up to 25 episodes in under a year, Dan insists that parts of it are no-brainers for him: "The dialogue is pretty easy for me. Everybody knows what the show is. We just don't know the exact

The *iCarly* set from the producer's point of view. Multi-tasker extraordinaire, Dan's working on a different scene than the one that's being filmed.

often completely blows me away (in a GREAT way) by taking some line of dialogue and delivering it with a hilarious twist I never would have thought of. I love it when that happens!" Since the show is written by a bunch of adults, occasionally they need some input from Miranda, Jennette, or Nathan. "Sometimes writers will come up and ask questions about certain words to make sure that kids, you know, still say that," Miranda told *Entertainment Weekly*. "We always crack about it because they'll say 'wonderful' in sentences that maybe kids these days wouldn't say." All these changes are incorporated into the final "Shooting Draft," the version of the script that will actually be used for filming.

On Thursday, the cameras finally get

everything is going as planned; he's also there to support his cast and make sure they're treated well. When he was a young actor on the late-'80s sitcom *Head of the Class*, he had first-hand experience being treated poorly on set. "Basically we were considered props who spoke," he related. He's also there to laugh at his own jokes, but it's not because he's full of himself — it turns out that's a way to help out the young cast as well. "The kids will forget to leave a beat [for laughter] after the jokes," he told the *New York Times*. "So I'm laughing to keep them from going too fast. If we're here until nine o'clock tonight, you'll still hear me laughing at the same jokes the same way." Writing duties plus his constant on-set presence often means 100-hour work weeks for Dan, who seems to be involved with every aspect of the production. Just ask Jerry, who confirms that Dan's "the show-runner in a very literal sense. He's there morning and night, writing scripts and giving notes to the directors. He is ever-present."

But does this mean that the actors work 100-hour weeks too? Well, labor laws say that actors under 18 can't work for more than nine and a half hours a day. But in between rehearsals and shooting, they still have to find time for school! There's a classroom right on the set, and an on-set teacher, and the young cast learns pretty much the same material their regular-school friends do. But as they get older, it gets harder and harder to cram all the schoolwork into the gaps in their work schedule. "They're really

rolling and they keep filming until the end of the day Friday, when hopefully the whole thing will be finished. Usually the *iCarly* team can polish off an episode a week, although occasionally they'll finish the work week with a couple scenes "owing" to be completed later.

As his frequent video and photo posts online attest, Dan makes sure he's present for the two days of filming. He's not just an executive producer who needs to make sure

Miranda, Jennette, and Nathan practice their lines with dialogue coach Lane Napper.

strict on *iCarly* about making sure we get our school time in," says Jennette. "We have to average up to three hours a day of schoolwork, but that's not quite enough for the 11th grade. So most of the time I'm catching up on weekends, and we have a long commute from our house to a studio where we shoot, so I work on the way up and back from there as well."

When you factor in getting to set and going home in the evenings, the days get even longer. Nathan outlined his day for *Portrait Magazine*: "I usually get up around 5:30 a.m. in order to do some form of exercise. Then we work nine and a half hours per day five days a week. Each day, I have about three or more hours of travel time to and from the set in which I'm usually doing schoolwork or memorizing my script." That kind of multi-tasking is essential to get everything done.

For the *iCarly* stars, life is a lot busier than for your average teenager, so what makes it all worthwhile? The work is actually fun. "It's just a blast to get to come in to the set and say hi to everyone and work with the people you know," Miranda related. "After a few months it seems like everybody's family."

Nathan agrees that the set has the right vibe: "From the beginning, everybody just clicked really fast. I was even more surprised with the crew because they had all worked together already for four seasons of *Drake & Josh* so they all knew each other and we all just became part of the new family. It was really cool to have that immersion, we all got along really great and everything flowed."

And at *iCarly*, not only is the crew fun, but the cast gets to do stuff most of us only dream of. "I don't know who else besides us could say they've run over a microwave filled with toothpaste in a monster truck," quips Jennette. Sounds like a pretty good day at the office. Or take some of Miranda's tweets: "Just finished filming the last scene of the week lol who knew rolling around in feathers could be so much fun?" or "I've been in a harness all day! Hanging in the air haha" or "This morning I worked with a baby pig, a ferret, a dog, two guinea pigs, and a parrot. I feel like Doctor Dolittle. I wish haha."

Everyone on set brings tons of energy, which is necessary to keep up with the hectic shooting schedule. "Filming an episode

The World of Schneider's Bakery: Dan Schneider knows a real "Socko," a "gifted furniture and cabinet maker" who created much of the wood furniture in his home.

Episode 8: "iSpy a Mean Teacher"

Original Air Date: November 3, 2007

The *iCarly* team decides to do a show on what mean teachers do outside of school, but Carly and Freddie get trapped in Ms. Briggs's closet, and Sam tries to help them escape.

Guest Star: J.R. Nutt plays Jim, the viewer with Connie (Samantha Aisling) who turns off the webcast. Nutt has appeared in several shows, starring as Kubrick in *Runaway Stars* and as Alexander, the café owner, in Disney's *Cory in the House.*

Fave Lines: Ms. Briggs: "I could have you expelled. I might even call the police." Sam: "Or you could just let us run away while you angrily shake your fist in the air and scream, 'You rotten kids!'"

iKnowledge: Carly says, "Let's sing her a public-domain birthday song" because "Happy Birthday to You" is actually owned by the Warner Music Group, and anyone singing the song on television has to pay Warner — until 2030 when the song enters the public domain. Ms. Briggs's original

composition, "Haggis and Moonlight," is really the famous Scottish song "Scotland the Brave." The black-and-white bunny footage is of Cookie, Dan Schneider's rabbit. **Did You Notice?:** In the first scene, there's a PTA poster, which pops up on various school walls in various episodes. If you were extremely allergic to bees like Freddie, would you be swatting at one? Cuttlefish is back again: Tareen spots Mr. Stern at the made-up band's concert.

On the Webcast: Ms. Briggs plays the bagpipes in front of a green screen while funny video footage plays behind her.
The World of Schneider's Bakery: Randy-Yos (now with 30% more Yos!) is a send-up of Cheerios. Jim calls the webcast "suckish," which is a word often used on *Drake & Josh* and *Zoey 101*.

Episode 9: "iWill Date Freddie"
Original Air Date: November 10, 2007

Freddie goes on a date with Valerie. She convinces him to be her tech producer, not *iCarly*'s.

Guest Star: Played by Mary Scheer, Freddie's mom gets some great scenes in this episode. Scheer has been on many television shows, including three seasons writing and acting on *MADtv*.

Fave Line: "She's always putting me down and calling me mean names, and every time I get an ice cream cone, she takes it and she licks it. She just licks it all over the place just to bug me." — Freddie, talking about Sam

iKnowledge: One piece of music played in the first-date scene was "Your New Boyfriend" by The Orion Experience.

Did You Notice?: Ridgeway is both a middle school (grades 6-8) and a high school (grades 9-12), one adjacent to the other. Carly, Freddie, and Sam are in the eighth grade, and Valerie's in ninth. But the banner on her locker reads RMS for Ridgeway *Middle* School, when she's in *high* school. When Jeremy turns the video camera around to introduce himself, you can see his wrist, which would be impossible if he was really holding the camera.

On the Webcast: Carly and Sam pretend to play guitar; there are two BlabCam bits; in "Animals Dressed Like Other Animals" a dog's dressed like a pig; and, during the credits, the request goes out for "crazy sandwich" pictures.

The World of Schneider's Bakery: No such luck, Valerie! TheValerieShow.com takes browsers to iCarly.com. Instead of Girl Scouts selling Thin Mints, Girl Sprouts sell Twin Mints in the iCarlyverse.

Episode 10: "iWant a World Record"

Original Air Date: November 17, 2007

To get into the *Jonas Book of World Records*, the team sets out to do the longest webcast (24 hours and 8 minutes) while Spencer builds a new sculpture with 137 moving parts.

Guest Stars: Brendan Patrick Connor plays the substitute teacher, Mr. Buttburn. Connor has acted in numerous TV shows and movies, including *ER* as Reidy. Bree Michael Warner, who plays Marilyn Raymer, the woman from Jonas, has appeared on a variety of TV series, including an episode of *Six Feet Under* specifically written for her! She's also a rock-music photographer.

Fave Lines: Freddie: "I could talk about dual-density memory chips, the importance of backing up your personal data." Sam: "I'd like to back up over your personal data with a truck."

iKnowledge: The record for the longest continuous webcast is reportedly 64 hours! It's true what Carly says: in the "Fitness American Style" survey, only 33% of respondents said that they enjoyed exercise. Blintzes can have any filling, not just soft cheese.

Did You Notice?: The clip used in the opening credits of *iCarly* of the gang having their photo taken for the Jonas book is not the same take that's used in the episode. (Check out Sam's smile in both.)

On the Webcast: Lots of segments for the marathon webcast: Random Dancing, "Street Fishing," "Tech Time with Freddie," "Fun with Bacon," the boy who tickles himself, the girls give each other "make overs" and dunk their heads in ice water, Carly's granddad pops by, and the grand finale is Spencer's Supertastic Sculpture of Stuff.

The World of Schneider's Bakery:

The *Jonas Book of World Records* is a parody of the famous *Guinness Book of World Records*.

Episode 11: "iRue the Day"

Original Air Date: December 1, 2007

After Spencer saves the life of Tom Higgenson of the Plain White T's, the band agrees to play on *iCarly*. But Nevel Papperman hacks into Freddie's computer to take control of the webcast.

Guest Stars: The Plain White T's are the stars of this episode, performing "Our Time Now" from their 2007 album *Every Second Counts*. That album also features "Hey There Delilah," their biggest hit to date. Family friend Colonel Morgan is played by Christopher Duncan, who played Braxton on *The Jamie Foxx Show*, Sergeant Ray Cutter on *The District*, and Clarence Wiedman on *Veronica Mars*. Just like Carly's, Duncan's father was an officer in the U.S. Air Force.

The Plain White T's are composed of Tom Higgenson (lead vocals, acoustic guitar), Dave Tirio (lead guitar), Tim G. Lopez (rhythm guitar), Mike Retondo (bass), and De'Mar Hamilton (drums).

Fave Line: "I have a webshow that I do, it is really bad. It's so dumb and boring too, it makes people sad . . ." — Nevel, singing to the tune of "Old MacDonald Had a Farm"

iKnowledge: The maroon beret worn by Colonel Morgan suggests that he and his men are Pararescuemen, a unit of the U.S. Air Force trained for search and rescue, also known as PJs.

Did You Notice?: Dan's bunny Cookie is among the images in Nevel's nerd cave. Nevel's living room must have a cathedral ceiling, because a *Mission: Impossible*–style cable harness couldn't be set up from a normal ceiling. And why does Freddie fall when Carly cuts only one of the cables, leaving two cables still attached? Colonel Morgan tells Nevel that he violated the Internet Security Act of 1983, but it wasn't actually passed until April 2000.

On the Webcast: The singing cat video is interrupted by a boy on a hobbyhorse; to cover for the technical mishap, they show a photo of an old lady biting a brick. Sam texts with her toes before Random Dancing kicks in — and Nevel takes over the webcast.

The World of Schneider's Bakery: Carly and Sam call their viewers Internetalonians and Webites.

Episode 12:
"iPromise Not to Tell"

Original Air Date: January 12, 2008
After Carly's history teacher gives her a B, Sam changes the grade in the principal's computer to give Carly straight As. Carly and Freddie try to change it back.

Guest Stars: Adrian Neil plays history teacher Mr. Devlin; Neil has had recurring roles as Liddy in *24* and as Nigel in *State of Grace*, and once played a vampire in *Buffy the Vampire Slayer*. Principal Franklin's secretary is played by Debi Derryberry, who is well known to Nickelodeon viewers as the voice of Jimmy Neutron. Derryberry has done lots of voice work in TV and movies, such as *Horton Hears a Who*, and video games, playing Coco Bandicoot in the *Crash Bandicoot* series.

Fave Lines: Carly: "Are you going to take us to juvie?" Freddie: "I don't want to go to juvie!" Carly: "They're going to take us to juvie!" Both: "Ooooooooh!"

iKnowledge: Videos of ankle-shaking — which is the type of promise Sam made Carly do — now appear frequently on YouTube. The guys from the Computer Security Agency broke into the Shays' apartment without showing a warrant. If Spencer had gone to law school for more than three days, he would have sued them rather than offered them punch.

Did You Notice?: Instructions in Japanese would be a mixture of scripts; Carly wouldn't be able to read out *rampu* for lamp. Principal Franklin has photos behind his desk in this episode; he had university degrees in the pilot, but one had his first name as Carl, not Ted! And is he the principal of Ridgeway High School or Ridgeway Junior High? (Or both?) When Freddie and Carly hack into the school's network, the screen says high school, but the CSA agent asks if they're in junior high.

On the Webcast: Carly freaks out and cuts the show short. During the credits, Sam votes *iCarly* the number one web show in the world.

The World of Schneider's Bakery: All of the computers in the classroom are older Apple iMacs, with the apple-shaped logo covered by a pear symbol. Pear computers also appear in *Zoey 101* and *Drake & Josh*. In the real world, a T5 jack is called a T1 jack.

Episode 13: "iAm Your Biggest Fan"

Original Air Date: January 19, 2008

The gang invites a huge fan of *iCarly* to be the first live audience member, but Mandy overstays her welcome.

Guest Stars: Aria Wallace plays obsessed fan Mandy Valdez. Aria is also a singer, and the star of the four Roxy Hunter movies shown on Nickelodeon. In the band Backflesh, Jon Seminara plays Blake, John Charles Meyer plays Dirk, and Kimberly Barnett plays Suezay. All three also appear as a band in a *Zoey 101* TV movie, along with Brandi Cyrus (Miley's older sister).

Fave Line: "I went to the junkyard. I have an account there." — Spencer

iKnowledge: When Spencer is listening to Backflesh after they kick him out, it's actually the band Backhouse Mike playing "Take Me Back," which is on the first *iCarly* soundtrack. Mandy says she went to Nordic Town, and there really is a Nordic Heritage Museum in the Ballard neighborhood in Seattle. The word on the Fladoodles bag, *deilig*, means delicious in Norwegian.

Did You Notice?: Mandy likes lots of types of berries, but not Halle Berry, the movie actor. So many things Spencer touches burst into flame: the homemade lava lamp, the police light on the car seats, and the cymbal.

On the Webcast: Another segment, "Twister Vision," debuts, as does the Spencer-built Seat of Sitting. Messin' with Lewbert is back, joining "Celebrity Armpit" and the "Spit Take" on the show. During the credits, Ashton flings himself in the air and onto a mat.

The World of Schneider's Bakery: The girls watch *Girly Cow*, which ran for at least four (imaginary) seasons, and it's the very same episode that appeared on *Drake & Josh* and *Zoey 101*. Bandana Republic is a take-off on Banana Republic.

Episode 14: "iHeart Art"

Original Air Date: February 2, 2008

Carly invites Spencer's idol, Harry Joyner, to look at his sculptures. When Joyner calls them "amateurish at best," Spencer decides to give up art. Meanwhile, Sam has to resist insulting Freddie for a whole week.

Guest Stars: Oliver Muirhead plays sculptor Harry Joyner. Muirhead has appeared in many television shows, including *The Suite Life* and *NCIS*. Bob Glouberman plays Dr. Moonie, the dentist; he recently appeared in *JONAS* as the brothers' vice-principal.

Fave Line: "Freddie, you didn't sign the Shampoo Agreement. How do I know if you double-pooed?" — Mrs. Benson

Jennette channelling Sam, as she considers how to dump this green stuff for some bacon!

beat-boxes while he plays the flute. Freddie and Spencer join the girls to plug the website during the credits.

The World of Schneider's Bakery: Mrs. Benson brings over Chips A Soy!, a play on Chips Ahoy! cookies. Freddie wants to dress up as Nug Nug for the convention; Dan's *Star Wars/Star Trek* parody, *Galaxy Wars*, was also mentioned on *Drake & Josh* and *Zoey 101*.

Episode 15: "iHate Sam's Boyfriend"

Original Air Date: February 9, 2008

Sam gets a boyfriend for the first time since fifth grade (and just in time for Nickelodeon's Crush Week) and ignores everyone else.

Guest Star: Aaron Albert plays Jonah in his first major TV role.

Fave Line: "Forget it. I gotta go squirt cheese down Gibby's pants before class. Hey, Gibby. Don't you run, Gibby!" — Sam

iKnowledge: Spencer is pretty close with his math for his claymation movie, *The Alien, the Space Hamster, and the Burrito.* A standard film has 24 frames per second so a 10-minute film would have 14,400 frames. If Spencer has 14,367 shots to go when Carly and Freddie interrupt him, then Spencer has only done 33 frames so far — not quite 2 seconds.

Did You Notice?: Freddie still has some cheese on his right cheek and his nose when the French teacher in the chicken suit walks by. But in the next shot, his cheek and nose

Did You Notice?: The building with the dental office is Schneider's Medical Complex (named for Dan Schneider). A number of Spencer's sculptures have been in previous episodes like Splatter Man ("iLike Jake"), Video Squirrel ("iPilot"), and The Bottle Bot.

On the Webcast: The art show segment is accompanied by Sam's cousin, Greg, who

are cheese-free. In the same scene, check out the picture of Drake Bell on Sam's locker door! There's no such thing as the Seattle Arts Council; it's called the Fremont Arts Council. **On the Webcast:** The girls rehearse the wig bit and test out the Giant Fan That Blows Stuff. Liliana the Acrobat makes her *iCarly* debut as does the "Wedgie-Bounce."

Episode 16: "iHatch Chicks"

Original Air Date: February 23, 2008
Carly and Sam decide to hatch baby chicks on the web show for a science project. Six chicks escape the incubator, and they have three hours to find them before "bad things happen."

Guest Stars: Doug Brochu plays Duke, who's teamed up with Freddie for the science project. Doug was in three earlier episodes of *iCarly*, once as a sweaty wrestler. Doug can be seen on *Sonny with a Chance* as Grady Mitchell.

Fave Line: "I wouldn't eat baby chicks . . . raw." — Sam

iKnowledge: When Spencer is caught in the duct, he shouts about "roly poly," which is usually used to describe someone who is round about the stomach. (The perfect shape for getting stuck in a duct.) But it can refer to anything that's spherical — is Spencer afraid of rolling dust bunnies?!

Did You Notice?: After Duke head-butts the wall, you can see the drywall in the apartment is made of paper. Spencer's hands are at his waist in the duct, even though they were at his shoulders when he went in.

On the Webcast: The girls play with the green screen; for the egg-themed episode there's a video of the guy in a bathtub full of scrambled eggs, and the girls introduce the incubating eggs. At the end, the girl pretends a string is pulling the corners of her mouth.

The World of Schneider's Bakery: Instead of drinking Coca-Cola, Sam is drinking Cabot-Cola. Both ZapLook.com, a search engine, and worldofchucks.com, the website devoted to people named Chuck, lead back to iCarly.com. The props department did an awesome job on the screen shot; there was even a little pear in the top left of the screen to match the logo on the laptop.

> "I'm not claustrophobic exactly, but I was in this enclosed box with my arms by my side, so even if I did freak out, there was no way to get out. It was very hot on the set, and when the chicks would get scared they would poop, and that smelled horrible. And the little chicks were right in my face. Like, right up my nose."
>
> — Jerry on the joys of filming "iHatch Chicks"

Episode 17: "iDon't Want to Fight"

Original Air Date: March 1, 2008
On their fifth friendship anniversary, Carly

gives Sam an *iCarly* T-shirt she made, but Sam trades the T-shirt to get Carly Cuttlefish tickets, sparking a huge fight.

Guest Stars: After four appearances, this episode marks the last (at least for seasons 1 and 2) of "Germy" Jeremy, played by Nathan Pearson, but the first appearance of Rip-off Rodney, played by Christopher David.

Fave Lines: Sam: "You know what else I got?" Freddie: "Pimples on your butt?"

iKnowledge: Spencer's automatic fish feeder is a classic Rube Goldberg machine. Goldberg was an American cartoonist and sculptor, and his character, Professor Lucifer Gorgonzola Butts, created machines like the one Spencer builds. Dan Schneider called the flashback where Carly and Sam meet over a tuna sandwich "a really cute scene." Rodney has tickets to Flaming Teeth, a play on the real-life band Flaming Lips, and to Backflesh, the band Spencer was briefly the drummer for ("iAm Your Biggest Fan").

Did You Notice?: Freddie's countdown goes from eight minutes to four minutes in about 45 seconds. Rodney has the same locker in this episode that Duke had in "iLike Jake." Carly and Sam open their lockers at the same time, but neither one actually unlocked them. Even though Freddie's not operating the camera, the framing and shot changes as the girls tell their side of the fight on the webcast.

On the Webcast: Chris and Chris, the meat drummers, get on the webcast as does the little girl surprising her mom in a present. Freddie ties up the girls' ponytails and tries

to end their fight. During the end credits, the boy bounces balls down the stairs.

Episode 18: "iPromote Tech-Foots"
Original Air Date: March 15, 2008

The *iCarly* team signs a lucrative contract to promote Tech-Foots, a new high-tech shoe, not realizing the sneakers have serious problems. Meanwhile, Spencer tries to find a new means of transportation after public transit takes him to Vancouver.

Guest Stars: Kevin Symons plays Greg Horvath, president of Daka Shoes. Symons starred as Dr. Kevin Adams on Discovery Kids' *Darcy's Wild Life*. Sam's personal chef, Sonya, was played by Liza Del Mundo, who's been on *W.I.T.C.H.* and *ER*.

Fave Line: "I'm their lawyer, and *this* is my necktie." — Spencer

iKnowledge: The Daka Shoe Company building is actually the Seattle Central Library, a glass-and-steel building voted one of America's favorites by the American Institute of Architects. The original title of this episode was "iGot a Sponsor."

Did You Notice?: Freddie says that 355,000 is the largest audience the webcast ever had, but in "iSpy a Mean Teacher," Freddie said it was 500,000. In "iPromise Not to Tell," Spencer asked Carly if she needed a ride to school and he drove her to Nevel's house in "iNevel," but in this episode, Spencer doesn't have a car. The helmet Spencer wears when he rollerblades is his dance helmet from "iDream of Dance."

On the Webcast: After earnestly promoting the shoes, Sam and Carly take sarcasm to new heights as they describe the Tech-Foots' "unique" properties.

The World of Schneider's Bakery: Carly gets an email on her PearPhone, a stand-in for Apple's iPhone. Daka Shoes were also in *Drake & Josh: Really Big Shrimp*. DiVoglio, the fictional best laptop ever, has now become synonymous with a dream computer in the real world. Mercedes Lens is a pun on luxury car company Mercedes-Benz.

Episode 19: "iGot Detention"

Original Air Date: March 22, 2008
Sam's detention conflicts with the *iCarly* 50th Webshow Spectacular!, so Carly and Freddie bring the webcast to the school's detention room.

Guest Stars: Veteran actor David St. James plays the mean teacher, Mr. Howard. St. James played congressman Darren Gibson on *The West Wing*. Claire, the lookout, is played by Erica Beck, who voiced Pearl, the octopus, in *Finding Nemo*. Colin Spensor plays beat-boxing Wesley, who finally gets a lengthier scene. Besides Gibby, Wesley has appeared in more *iCarly* episodes than any other classmate character.

Fave Lines: Sam: "Is that thing filled with coffee?" Spencer: "Oh, just about 500 gallons."

iKnowledge: Dan Schneider is a huge fan of Larry David, who popularized (with writer Larry Charles) the Atomic Wedgie on *Seinfeld* (where the waistband goes over the head). In this episode, Schneider (with

writer Andrew Hill Newman) popularizes the Texas Wedgie, where the underwear is yanked so fast, it smokes. The tool that Carly can't name is a ratchet.

Did You Notice?: The microwave that catches on fire is the same one — 1100 watts! — that Carly and Freddie gave Principal Franklin in "iPromise Not to Tell." Mr. Howard's mouth healed quickly! The

day after he was wearing a brace, he could yell again. Carly says there are three minutes of school left, but the final bell rings a minute later.

On the Webcast: The 50th Webshow Spectacular! features the cap cam worn by classmate Billy, Turtle Races, and the boy who plays the *iCarly* theme while his feet are behind his head.

The World of Schneider's Bakery: Carly stole Freddie's fruit-scented Mr. Smelly markers, which are made by Mr. Sketch in the real world. Sam has to read *Scarlett's Web*, not the classic by E.B. White, *Charlotte's Web*.

Episode 20: "iStakeout"

Original Air Date: April 5, 2008

After noticing the street view on an *iCarly* webcast, two cops use the Shays' apartment to watch a convenience store across the street that they suspect sells pirated DVDs. One cop, who used to bully Spencer at camp, renews his terrorizing of Spencer.

Guest Stars: Curtis Armstrong plays the store clerk and is probably best known to older audiences as "Booger" Dawson in the *Revenge of the Nerds* movies and to younger audiences as The Zit in an episode of *Wizards of Waverly Place*. Armstrong has also had regular roles on *Boston Legal* and

The World of Schneider's Bakery: The gang dines at The Cheesecake Warehouse, rather than The Cheesecake Factory. whynotdateme.com, the dating website, circles back to iCarly.com. Celine and Julia go to see *Girly Cow on Ice.* (Sam and Carly watched *Girly Cow* in "iAm Your Biggest Fan.")

Penny Tees: Spencer wears "Pump Up the Fruit," a line Sam said before exploding the watermelon in "iCarly Saves TV."

Episode 25:
"iHave a Lovesick Teacher"

Original Air Date: July 25, 2008

After the gang's history teacher breaks up with her boyfriend, she decides to take it out on her students until Spencer and the teacher begin dating. But when he breaks up with her too, it's up to the *iCarly* team to find a way to stop their teacher from failing them altogether.

Guest Stars: Jessica Makinson plays Lauren Ackerman, the lovesick history teacher. Makinson appeared on Comedy Central's *Halfway Home, Trigger Happy TV*, and in the second season of *The Joe Schmo Show*, the reality TV show parody on Spike TV. She also did voice work on *South Park*, another of Dan Schneider's favorite shows. Ashley Argota has a brief appearance, telling the gang why Miss Ackerman is upset; Ashley now stars on *True Jackson, VP* as Lulu.

Fave Line: "Oh look, more backtalk from the sassmaster." — Miss Ackerman

iKnowledge: This episode aired with "iWin a Date" in an *iCarly* Double Date

date either run out crying or flee when Gibby starts dancing, Gibby got stuck paying the bill!

On the Webcast: In the 10-second paint-off, Carly paints a clown on Gibby's front, and Sam paints a meatball on Gibby's back. The "I Win a Date" segment is quite similar to the classic TV show *The Dating Game*. And don't forget Samantha, who makes animal noises.

Spencer vs. Goldfish

Goldfish of Seattle: steer clear of the Shay residence! In "iLike Jake," Spencer accidentally eats his goldfish; in "iDon't Want to Fight," goldfish Reggie and Swimmy die because Spencer forgot to feed them, a tank fires at goldfish Brock and then Spencer almost drinks him. In "iCarly Saves TV," Spencer throws a baseball and kills a goldfish. Spencer tells Miss Ackerman in "iHave a Lovesick Teacher" that he has a goldfish, but they're just friends.

Night. Spencer's favorite animals are pigs and panda bears. Illegally downloading songs is a violation of the U.S. Digital Millennium Copyright Act, and carries a penalty of up to three years in prison and $250,000 in fines.

Did You Notice?: As Spencer is about to carve the chicken, he quickly pulls something white off the top of it that appears to be the shaving cream prop used in the earlier scene. Miss Ackerman makes the gang do jumping jacks as punishment for talking back, but in "iGot Detention," Sam says that Principal Franklin doesn't allow physical punishment. Freddie wonders at the end of the episode if they should tell Principal Franklin, but the FBI officers would have had to get Franklin's permission before making the arrest on school property.

On the Webcast: The segment "Make Up or Break Up," to determine whether Spencer and Miss Ackerman should still date, got 257,804 votes for a break up. During the end credits, a boy wakes up his dad with ping-pong balls.

The World of Schneider's Bakery: The PearPod is back; if only Miss Ackerman had bought her 500 songs from PearTunes. . . .

Penny Tees: Carly is in a Penny Tee that reads "Parole Baby."

★ SEASON 2 ★

Episode 26: "iSaw Him First"

Original Air Date: September 27, 2008

Both Sam and Carly see and crush on Freddie's friend, Shane, at the exact same moment. Under the "girl code," they decide they should both go out with him, but it gets competitive.

Guest Stars: James Maslow stars as Shane in his first major TV role, and now plays James on Nick's *Big Time Rush*. Marilyn Sue Perry plays the school nurse with the paddles. Perry also performs in cabaret and musical comedy, sings gospel, and teaches acting.

Fave Lines: Sam: "Why does your voice sound deeper?" Freddie: "I don't know . . . puberty?"

iKnowledge: A "smoker" is a fog machine, which vaporizes a special fluid ("fog juice" made out of a water-, glycol-, or glycerin-based liquid) blown from the machine that condenses into fog when it hits the outside air. The tune during the credits is Miranda's hit "Stay My Baby." This was the first episode to have an "extended version," featuring deleted scenes; Nickelodeon aired it on the Wednesday following Saturday's regular version.

Did You Notice?: When Carly kisses Shane, she claims she wins, but the rules were clear: Shane had to kiss her.

On the Webcast: Lots of insanity on *iCarly* this episode: speed-walking and hula time, blueberries up the girls' noses, and trombone and idiot hula dancing. With

James Maslow of *Big Time Rush* plays nice with Miranda after a street hockey face off as fierce as Sam and Carly's battle for Shane.

Shane, his Magno-Static Multi-Pulse Flux Generator, vinegar, goat's milk, a crystal rod, and their tongues, Carly and Sam have "Fun with Magnetism."

Penny Tees: Sam might want to borrow Freddie's "Electric Ham" shirt.

Episode 27: "iStage an Intervention"

Original Air Date: October 4, 2008

Spencer finds an old Pak-Rat game, becomes obsessed with getting the all-time

make a baby laugh, the gang takes him for his first piece of Mr. Galini's pie. After Mr. Galini dies, the gang fears his recipes are lost.

Guest Stars: Jim Pirri plays Mario, the faithful pie-store worker; Pirri appeared on *Zoey 101*, *Providence*, and *Chuck*.

Fave Line: "Mmm, why can't I marry this pie? All I want out of life is to be Mrs. Sam This Pie." — Sam

iKnowledge: Joe Catania's name is often seen in the end credits after Dan Schneider. Catania produced most episodes of *iCarly* and, working for Schneider's Bakery, has produced or co-produced many episodes of *Zoey 101*, *Drake & Josh*, and *All That*. He was production manager for *The Amanda Show*, and got his start on *The Cosby Show*, first as an assistant to the producers, and then as an associate producer.

Did You Notice?: Galini's Pie Shop is in a building called Schneider's Properties. The baby vomit on Freddie's bear costume changes throughout the scene. The fork in Carly's pie also moves from one shot to the next. The recipes go flying when Galini's computer is knocked to the floor, but when Carly bends over to grab them, they're back in the computer.

On the Webcast: The girls ask viewers to send in the best coconut cream pie recipes. A girl, Emma, opens her fridge door using her shoulder blade.

The World of Schneider's Bakery: "Fudgebag" is a popular insult on Dan's shows.

Penny Tees: Freddie is on "Pudding Patrol."

Episode 31: "iChristmas"

Original Air Date: December 13, 2008

Carly's disappointed that Spencer sculpted a Christmas tree out of junk instead of buying a real tree. When the tree catches on fire and destroys her presents, she wishes Spencer had been born normal, and an angel appears to grant her wish.

Guest Stars: Danny Woodburn plays Mitch the angel; Woodburn is best known

for his role as Mickey, Kramer's buddy, in *Seinfeld*. Dot Jones plays the juvie guard; she played Coach Kelly in Disney's *Lizzie McGuire*, and is a 15-time world arm-wrestling champion.

Fave Line: "And I want you to be my friend, and say, 'Five, four, three, two' but not the 'one,' which I never understood, but I liked it. And I just want my life back!" — Carly to Freddie

iKnowledge: This episode is inspired by the classic Frank Capra movie *It's a Wonderful Life*, and by *A Charlie Brown Christmas* (with the little tree). Carly says that Sam wears mismatched socks for good luck; Jennette McCurdy does this every day! There actually is a juvenile detention center in Seattle, but it's called the King County Youth Service Center.

Did You Notice?: In the *iCarly* studio,

their iWeb award is on the wall. We see Spencer's bedroom for the first time since "iDream of Dance." The king of clubs is at different angles from one shot to the next. Spencer mentions Mr. Schneider and Mr. Newman on the phone, an in-joke about Dan Schneider and Andrew Hill Newman, one of the show's writers.

On the Webcast: For the Christmas episode, Sam and Carly say "Merry Christmas" in a Challenger raft and Freddie dresses as a Christmas flashlight.

The World of Schneider's Bakery: Sam's favorite book, *Boogie Bear III: The Return of Boogie Bear*, gets another mention. (The first was in "iFence.")

Penny Tees: Spencer wears "Mister Duck Lumps."

Episode 32: "iKiss"

Original Air Date: January 3, 2009

After a prank war between Sam and Freddie, Sam reveals on the webcast that Freddie has never kissed a girl. Carly berates Sam for going too far, so Sam reveals that she has never kissed anyone either. Meanwhile, Spencer trains for a pro football try-out.

Fave Line: "Gibby's way worse than a dead fish." — Sam

iKnowledge: With frequent reruns on Nickelodeon, Dan doesn't like *iCarly* to have a strict timeline, because most viewers don't see the episodes in order. However, this episode shows that there is some sequence of events: Carly brings up last season's girl-friend, Valerie, from "iWill Date Freddie" and this episode is a set-up for the first episode of season 3. Also, Freddie listens to "Running Away," written and performed by AM, on his fire escape.

Did You Notice?: Have Freddie and Sam really never kissed anyone before? In "iWill Date Freddie," Freddie says he and Valerie

Seddie? Maybe.

have kissed "a little" and she gives him a peck on the lips, and in "iSaw Him First," Sam says that she "enjoys lips to lips." Seattle's professional football team is the Seahawks, not the Cobras. Spencer sends Gibby to Woodley Park, which is in Washington, D.C., not Seattle, Washington.

On the Webcast: Sam and Carly show the trailer for *Kelly Cooper: Terrible Movie* (rated T for Terrible); Sam spills Freddie's secret; the Meatball War (from boxes marked "Inexpensive Meatballs") is cut short; Sam confesses; there's a photo of the man with shrimp up his nose; and the boy plays basketball while riding a unicycle.

Penny Tees: Carly gets into "Cookie Mischief."

Episode 33: "iGive Away a Car"

Original Air Date: January 17, 2009

The son of a local car dealer convinces the gang to run a contest with a new car as the prize. Meanwhile, Spencer buys a replica cruiser from his favorite sci-fi movie, which comes in handy when the contest goes awry.

Guest Stars: Tom Beyer plays LCC Inspector Bullock. A veteran of stage and screen, Beyer spent several years in Seattle as a company member of Book-It Repertory Theater. Mike Grief, who plays one of the movers, appeared in two episodes of *The Amanda Show*.

Fave Line: "Yes, Little Larry Lies-A-Lot?" — Spencer to Freddie

iKnowledge: Being a haberdasher (Nevel's

dream) is a noble profession, once done by Harry S. Truman and Johnny Carson.

Did You Notice?: The pickle juice jar Sam drinks from is labeled "Schneider's," another sly reference to Dan. In the scene with Nevel in the hallway, watch Sam's hair move from take to take.

On the Webcast: There's the Special Contest with the give-away from Flanken Motors; George, the bra who tells ghost stories; and more Random Dancing.

The World of Schneider's Bakery: Spencer buys the proton cruiser from Craigsmix.com, a mash-up of Craigslist and eBay; the URL leads back to iCarly.com. First mentioned in an episode of *Drake & Josh* called "The Battle of Panthatar," *Galaxy Wars* is a mix of 1970s and '80s sci-fi references. The cruiser with its call sign of "Rouge IV ST49 3495" nods to *Star Wars* (red was Luke Skywalker's squadron's call sign). The communicator that Spencer uses is classic *Star Trek*. The LCC is a stand-in for the FCC, the Federal Communications Commission. One of the movers says he's reading *The Sisters Who Had Magic Pants* in his book club, which is Schneider's version of *The Sisterhood of the Traveling Pants*.

Penny Tees: Sam wears a "My Cheese, My Rules" tee.

Episode 34: "iRocked the Vote"

Original Air Date: February 7, 2009

Carly and Sam encourage viewers to vote for David Archuleta on *America Sings*, and time "Happy Birthday to You" hasn't been sung on *iCarly*. (The first time was in "iSpy a Mean Teacher.") Freddie says, "It's not P.D."; P.D. means public domain, as Dan mentioned in his Fun Facts for this episode. Dan Schneider revealed that the closing credits scene isn't set in Freddie's actual bedroom; it's simply a dream.

Did You Notice?: Pete tells Sam that he'll text her; does he already have Sam's number? This is the first episode where "DanWarp" is part of the logo at the end of the show.

On the Webcast: On "I'd Morph That," Carly's head is combined with Sam's rabid cat. Sam's birthday party is broadcast to the web world.

The World of Schneider's Bakery: El Taco Guapo is kind of like Taco Bell; there really is an El Guapo restaurant in Los Angeles that has Taco Tuesdays! Hey Food is a parody of grocery store chain Whole Foods.

Penny Tees: Freddie has "Squirrel Germs."

Episode 39: "iGo Nuclear"

Original Air Date: April 22, 2009

For science class, the gang has to come up with a unique project to benefit the environment. When Carly's project fails to impress the teacher, Spencer enlists the help of a new friend to get her an A+.

Guest Stars: Andrew Hill Newman not only co-wrote this episode, but plays Mr. Henning, the hippie science teacher. Newman has guest starred on a slew of TV series, including *Star Trek: Voyager* (with Tim "Principal Franklin" Russ) and *Zoey 101*. Lauren Benz Phillips plays Gibby's mom; she was also in an episode of *Drake & Josh* and *Wizards of Waverly Place*.

Fave Lines: Cal: "This is a pepperoni stick." Spencer: "Oh my God, I'm in trouble."

iKnowledge: The original title for this episode was "iGo Green"; Dan wrote about naming episodes in his Fun Facts for "iGo Nuclear." On the National Green Week calendar is Ed Begley Jr., actor and environmental activist, who is on the board of directors of the Environmental Media Association. The shot of the Seattle skyline was taken from the south. Bushwell Plaza may be on the west side of Seattle, but it should be fairly close to downtown, because the downtown buildings of Seattle, including the Space Needle, are right outside the big window on the main floor. The police officer says that Cal imports uranium rods, but the case read "Плутоний," which means plutonium in Russian. Officer Price calls in a "10-41"; in California, 10-41 is the code for going on duty.

Did You Notice?: A different entrance to Ridgeway High School is shown in the opening. Freddie and Carly are still in the same clothes as when they got the assignment when he shows his Portuguese worms, even though it is much later. The distance the kid on the tricycle is past Carly varies from shot to shot. When Sam squeezes the orange juice into her mouth, she dribbles it in her eye and on her cheek and neck. (And she eats that whole orange in about five seconds.) At the Groovy Smoothie after the web cast, Carly bumps her elbow and quietly says, "Ow. Jeez." The closing credits segment is the same one used in "iMeet Fred."

On the Webcast: Special guests for Green Week include Cal in sunglasses so he's not recognized. In addition to the generator, there's Strobe Lights and Random Strobing.

Penny Tees: Spencer wears the tee in this episode, "Butter Me Queasy."

Episode 40: "iDate a Bad Boy"

Original Air Date: May 9, 2009

A new guy in the apartment building steals Spencer's motorcycle. At first Carly dislikes Griffin, but it doesn't take long for her to fall for him. Sam hires Freddie to program her website.

Guest Stars: Drew Roy plays Griffin. Drew played bad-boy Jesse in a two-part episode of *Hannah Montana*, and Travis Benjamin in ABC's *Lincoln Heights*. David Hadinger plays the monster; he played a monster on an episode of *All That* as well.

Fave Line: "Whee! Don't break up with us, Carly! Love us. We can all get married. And honeymoon on Pee Wee Island! The sand on the beach is made of sugar. Whee! Whee!" — the Pee Wee Babies

iKnowledge: Griffin annoys Carly with "New Fast Song" by Teaneck from *Masters of Achievement*. Carly mentions that Spencer won't give her an allowance unless she wears the lame clothes; that allowance comes from Colonel Shay who gives Spencer money for Carly's food, clothes, books, and more. If Sam and Freddie really did draw up a contract through a lawyer, there would have been two copies of it. Eric Goldberg, one of the *iCarly* writers, actually had this nightmare of a monster eating his soup.

Did You Notice?: When Spencer turns on the lights in the living room, Griffin and Carly don't even react. Carly picks up the sledgehammer that Spencer was using, but it's not the same one. (Read Dan's Fun Facts to find out why.) Spencer's Bottle Bot must have mechanical parts, since its red eyes can dilate — it's the one electrical thing that Spencer builds that doesn't catch on fire. When Sam and Carly play the videogame, there's a glimpse of the Shays' "fourth wall." The video in the closing credits is the same one used in "iLook Alike" and "iHurt Lewbert."

On the Webcast: Sam and Carly give Alex a bad haircut; they have an argument over vanilla and chocolate; Matt and Clifford eat snowflakes; and raisins rain down on Carly and Sam.

The World of Schneider's Bakery: Sham-Pow, the miracle cloth, is a play on the Sham-Wow. Pee Wee Babies are collectible stuffies much like Beanie Babies. Some of the props used as Pee Wee Babies are actually Beanie Babies; Stretch the Ostrich and Rocket the Blue Jay are on the shelf. Sam's website, www.sampuckett.com, circles back to iCarly.com.

Penny Tees: Two tees in one episode!

Jennette, Ryan Ochoa, Jake T. Austin, and Mitchel Musso at the Sweet 16 Party for *Wizards of Waverly Place*'s Jennifer Stone.

money for charity, Carly reluctantly agrees to fight Shelby Marx, the new women's MMA champion. Trash talking, an injured grandma, and Nevel Papperman complicate the bout. Spencer takes an allergy medication with five bad side effects.

Guest Stars: Sean Smith plays Dr. Dresdin from apartment 10G; Smith has guest starred on tons of TV shows, including *24* and *CSI*.

Fave Moment: Spencer repeatedly whacking Gibby's popcorn in the air and Gibby's reactions.

iKnowledge: "iFight Shelby Marx" was watched by almost 8 million viewers. When Carly is fighting Shelby, she does a little Three Stooges routine. The ads at the CFC fights include Hurt Machine, Carnage Cage, Hostile Evolution, Bone Snap (Sam has its logo on her laptop), and Bludgeon Cologne. Shelby Marx's brand is Pink Bull. Carly spots Sir Mix-a-Lot in the crowd. A Seattle-based rap artist, his real name is Anthony Ray, and he won a Grammy for his song "Baby Got Back."

Did You Notice?: The amount of popcorn in Carly's bowl changes between shots. (Maybe this blooper is because the scene was so long, as Dan mentions in his Fun Facts for "iFight Shelby Marx.") In the scene where they watch the CFC at the Shays' apartment, the fourth wall is visible again, and this time there's a gumball machine and a set of croquet mallets. The press conference is at the Beverly Garvin Hotel, the same place where Nevel had his signing in "iWant My Website Back." The fight is held

Quisp Under 21 DANce Club ("DAN" for Dan Schneider).

Penny Tees: Freddie knows that "Fries Matter." (Dan reveals who else loves french fries in his Fun Facts for "iTwins.")

Episode 45: "iFight Shelby Marx"

Original Air Date: August 8, 2009

To generate publicity for the show and raise

Victoria Justice (Shelby Marx)

Born February 19, 1993, in Hollywood, Florida, Victoria Dawn Justice got her call to acting later than some of her costars, but quickly made up for lost time. Watching a children's commercial at age eight, Victoria decided it was something she could do too. It didn't take long to prove she was right, since Victoria's first gig was a national spot for Ovaltine, and more success quickly followed. In addition to commercials, Victoria also became an in-demand child model in South Beach. Both of these earlier accomplishments would grow along with Victoria: throughout her career she did dozens more commercials including ones for AOL, Mervyn's, Peanut Butter Toast Crunch, and the Los Angeles Dodgers, and she realized the dreams of aspiring models everywhere by landing campaigns for Gap, Guess, and Ralph Lauren.

Victoria's first dramatic role would be a one-line part on the mother-daughter drama *Gilmore Girls*, in which she dressed up as a hobbit in over 100 degree temperatures. After Victoria's initial crossover from commercials, she landed a lead role in 2005's indie short film *Mary*.

Things picked up for Victoria after a guest appearance on the Disney Channel hit *The Suite Life of Zack & Cody*. In 2005, she snagged spots in three films: horror/thriller *The Garden*, psychological thriller *Unknown*, and the CBS special *Silver Bells*.

But everything changed for Victoria when she landed the role of Zoey's roommate Lola Martinez on *Zoey 101*. Lola is a chatty aspiring actress who wants to win an Academy Award by age 19 — basically she wishes she had the kind of success Victoria's had so far.

Yet there was still more to come. In 2008, Victoria hit the big time, and on August 13, Nickelodeon announced that Victoria had been signed to an overall talent and music deal. Nick executive VP Paula Kaplan told the press, "She's a rare kind of actress. She's beautiful, yet takes a fearless approach to acting. Kids loved her on *Zoey 101* because she could boldly take a pie in the face or just as easily tackle a dramatic scene. It is this versatility combined with her musical talent and real-girl qualities that make her someone we are excited about." As if that wasn't enough, Columbia Records' Jay Landers spoke about her musical talents: "Besides her acting skills which are already well known to her fans, she has a terrific recording voice. When she steps up to the mic, her personality shines through."

Dan Schneider busily worked on making another hit show for his new star, which focuses on a talented young girl at a performing arts school, and began filming in 2009. When Dan puts his faith and creative energies behind an actor it's an amazing opportunity for young talent. The writer/producer told Victoria, "I can't give you a car for your Sweet 16 birthday, but as a gift, I can give you your own show." In preparation for *Victorious*, Victoria put in a guest appearance on *iCarly* as MMA superstar Shelby Marx, a role rumored to turn into a regular gig in *iCarly*'s third season. She can also be spotted on an episode of *True Jackson, VP*. Victoria also beefed up her film experience with two lead roles: starring alongside the Sprouse twins in the adventure/comedy *The Kings of Appletown*, and showcasing her singing skills in *Spectacular!*

With a career that's been successful from day one and is only getting bigger, it looks like Dan Schneider picked the perfect title for Victoria's new show, for this rising star is nothing if not "Victorious."

Victoria's zany talents could get her featured on iCarly.com: "I can pick up anything with my toes, including small things like pennies. And I can do the eyebrow wave, where I make my eyebrows move in a slow wave like the ocean. And this one is the weirdest ever. I'm really good at catching flies. My reflexes are good. I just lurk and get them."

at the Seattle Super Center; when the building was shown in "iLook Alike," its name wasn't on it. The clock during the Shelby Marx–Maya Feckner fight is impossibly slow; during the Marx–Shay fight, the timer continues after Carly calls a time-out. When Spencer asks the doctor several days later about the allergy medication, none of the pills have been taken (nor when he points them out to Carly later on). When Carly and Freddie watch videos on SplashFace, keep an eye out for the DanWarp video. The bunny picture Shelby holds up is of Dan's bunny, Cookie. On Nevelocity.com, the sponsor is Hungry Girl (Lisa Lillien's website). Daniel Kash is listed twice in the credits.

On the Webcast: Starting with Toes with 'Fros, there are tons of segments on this supersized episode: trash talking Shelby Marx; garbage cans as really bad underwear; Carly canceling the fight; Shelby Marx guest starring; the slow-motion grape juice spit-take; Random Dancing; and Carly feeding salsa to Baby Spencer during the end credits. That clip was used in a promo for the 2009 Teen Choice Awards.

The World of Schneider's Bakery: The send-up of the UFC (Ultimate Fighting Championship) is the CFC (Cross Fighting Championships). (In "iLook Alike," the sport was just referred to as MMA.) But the UFC doesn't have female fighters. Another league, Strikeforce, had its first women's championship on August 15, 2009 (a week after this episode aired) between Cristiane "Cyborg" Santos and Gina Carano. Dan Schneider said that Carano was the inspiration for Shelby Marx. The network broadcasting the Marx–Shay fight is TSBN, instead of ESPN. The announcers for the fight are Jack Schneider and Marvin Lillien, named for Dan Schneider and Lisa Lillien.

Penny Tees: For a very special episode, Freddie wears a "Special Ham" tee.

Jennette playing Santa at the Camp Ronald McDonald for Good Times Holiday Party in 2008. "Just to be able to help these kids in any way and see them smile — it's something I feel really blessed to be able to do," says the actress, who has participated in the event multiple times.

time so she watches it with her daughter. She told me that I was a great actress and very funny. I hugged her twice. It was just so amazing. Just talking about it sends shivers down my spine."

The Fame Game

When Miranda and her cast mates are compared to some other teen-actor success stories, there's always one thing missing:

scandal. While some struggle with achieving success so young, the *iCarly* actors have kept themselves out of the tabloids and gossip blogs. How do they keep their heads on straight? Miranda focuses on the relationships that matter: "I just like being with my friends and seeing movies and stuff. I don't have time to go crazy or anything." And although she certainly hangs out with other famous teens — aside from her *iCarly*

the studio, this time with what would become the debut single for her EP, *About You Now*. Whereas on the *iCarly* soundtrack Miranda merely helped pick the songs, this time she got involved in the writing. Although she doubted her songwriting ability at first, she got into the groove soon enough. "Ever since I started playing guitar when I was little I have always tried to write songs but I wasn't really sure about how good they were lol," she wrote on her blog. "When I first started writing with people for my CD I was really nervous about getting in there and telling them all my ideas. Now it's my favorite part!"

Luckily she has lots of people to support her with the songwriting process. She told *People*, "One of the songwriters I had been working with told me to keep a book, like a journal. So every time I have an idea or a fun experience, I write it down so I can remember. It's like a diary but with songs in mind. It actually works. I also play guitar. One of my best friends is really into music. She plays drums, and she'll come over to my house, and we'll write about some crazy thing that happened to her at school that day. And I write about boys. That's usually what most of the songs are about."

This contribution to the writing process would be the biggest change from Miranda's previous offerings; musically, the album would sound similar to her songs on the *iCarly* soundtrack. "It's still pop-rock, fun music like the *iCarly* soundtrack, but I think it's a little more mature. They're love songs

and just fun songs about hanging out with your girlfriends," explained Miranda. In a nutshell it's "fun, pop, rock-girl empowerment" music that reflects the influences of her favorite performers Gwen Stefani and Avril Lavigne. The album also had powerful producers to help Miranda fine tune her sound — the Matrix and Dr. Luke, who produced such pop sensations as Britney Spears and Kelly Clarkson.

The album was released February 3, 2009, featuring the title track and two new songs: "FYI," a rocker girl anthem about playing hard to get and going down in flames for love, and "Party Girl," a hard-driving song about a night out on the town with your friends. The EP also includes Spider remixes of "About You Now" and "Stay My Baby."

"About You Now," originally a song by the Sugababes released in 2007, is about a relationship that ended too soon. Miranda got the chance to perform the song live during the Macy's Thanksgiving Day Parade in 2008, as well as at the 2009 Kids' Choice Awards preshow. Between the *iCarly* soundtrack and the new EP, "About You Now" was Miranda's biggest hit so far, peaking at number 47 on the Billboard Hot 100.

After her success with the "Stay My Baby" video, Miranda got the chance to film another video, for "About You Now." When Miranda was deciding on a concept or "treatment" for her video, she knew she wanted a fairly straightforward interpretation that was true to the original song. The

Miranda cast her friends in her "About You Now" video: (left to right) Nina Nunden, Catarina Baraja, and Hayley Erina.

video, directed by Billie Woodruff (who's known for his R&B and hip hop videos), takes place in a mall, with Miranda remembering the relationship she had with an old boyfriend, who she still hasn't gotten over. For the budding pop star, one of the most fun parts of making this video was getting to cast six of her real-life best friends as her friends at the mall, making her time on set a blast. Miranda enthused, "We shot the video at a mall so we got to go shopping and hang out all day." She also got to help pick this video's heartthrob, Diego Gonzalez, a well-known Mexican singer and soap opera actor. Miranda also worked with the same band as in "Stay My Baby." She says the band is "super funny and always making jokes on set and being silly," and that they've sort of become her real band, since she rehearses a lot with them too. Miranda had a significant part in the creative process for this video. In a special behind-the-scenes video for *Pop Star Magazine*, the singer explained, "I figured out what I wanted to do, like the different moves I was going to do in the song . . . the choreographer came in and she helped me with all of it. And then they added the band in. So they came in and that made it fun because the energy was crazy and insane."

Although she had experience recording songs for soundtracks, Miranda got an opportunity to do her first song for a feature film, Sony's 2009 computer-animated release *Cloudy with a Chance of Meatballs*. Based on the kid's book classic of the same

name by Judy and Ron Barrett, *Cloudy* is about a well-intentioned but unsuccessful inventor (sounds a little like Spencer, doesn't it?) who finally gets his break when he invents a machine that turns water into food, and consequently saves his town from hunger when it starts raining breakfast, lunch, and dinner! He's celebrated — until the food that's been falling from the sky

takes on a life of its own. Miranda's single, "Raining Sunshine," was released on August 25, 2009, and is all about holding on to hope no matter what happens. It's "kind of inspirational and fun to listen to . . . it just makes me happy to sing it," says the singer.

Miranda got to make another video for this song, and just like with "About You Now," Miranda jumped at the chance to cast her real-life friends in the video. (This one features "The Hayleys," Haley Ramm and Hayley Erina, who also appeared in the "About You Now" video.) It starts with footage of Miranda in her room singing her heart out, spliced with scenes from the movie. But as the song picks up, a little of the movie creeps into Miranda's world, and when she holds a pot out the window, it's filled with raining spaghetti (hopefully for some spaghetti tacos!). Before the video is over, Miranda's rocking out with her band in the garage, and, just like in real life, it looks like it's raining sunshine for Miranda. Filming the video was a great time for Miranda, who called it "just a fun crazy day," adding, "When I'm doing *iCarly*, I have to learn lines. This was so laid-back."

Things have really taken off for Miranda's music career, and though she hasn't yet reached a Miley Cyrus level of success, the Nickelodeon star isn't concerned about being competitive. When asked what she thought of Miley, Miranda giggled and replied, "I like Hannah Montana. I have her CDs." For her, that kind of success is a goal, but she's not pitting herself against the Disney star. "I mean, Miley's so successful. I'd love to be able to go on tour and perform like her," she told the *LA Times*. "It just looks like so much fun."

That wish is coming true, and she shared on her website about getting ready to go on tour. In a blog entry, she wrote: "I have a few weeks off from *iCarly* so I have been rehearsing for hours and hours every day for when I go on tour! It's been really fun! I'm going over singing a lot of my songs from my upcoming cd as well as songs that are already out and working with a choreographer as well. It's a lot of work to sing and run around at the same time! I had no idea how much fun it would be though! I have been doing a lot of exercises also that help build up endurance so that it's easy to sing a lot of songs in a row. It's so exciting to know I'm going to get to go on tour and meet all of you guys and perform!" At the rate Miranda's star has been climbing, it's only a matter of time before she's on the road!

And after all this success, what's Miranda's advice for aspiring singers? "Practice a lot! I've been taking a lot of lessons since I was little. It's cool because you become more confident with yourself. It really helps! Even if it's just singing along with the radio." Singing in the shower can lead to pretty good things too!

chapter 15

Some Things Are Meant to Be

Nickelodeon's rising stars: Victoria Justice of *Victorious*, Miranda, and Keke Palmer of *True Jackson, VP.*

With *iCarly* in its third season, the cast is on fire (not literally . . . unless Spencer's been messing around) and it doesn't look like things will be cooling off any time soon. The show regularly draws almost 8 million viewers for new episodes, making it the highest rated show of all Nickelodeon and Disney shows, and often the number one scripted show on cable! Even the actors didn't predict huge numbers like these. "When we started the show, we had no idea that it was going to be this big," says Nathan. "Just the concept and the cast, and everything put together, we knew it was going to be a good show. But we didn't know it was going to be this big."

iCarly's genius is also being recognized with a smattering of awards including a 2009 Kids' Choice Award for Favorite TV show (following a nomination in 2008), a 2009 Teen Choice Award nomination for Choice TV Show–Comedy, and even a 2009 Emmy nomination for Outstanding Children's Program. The actors weren't forgotten either — both Jerry and Miranda were nominated for Teen Choice awards, and Miranda also got a nod at the Kids' Choice Awards.

So with success like this, can fans look forward to more *iCarly* goodness for a while? On his blog, Dan explained that there are several factors that go into deciding how long a show will run: ratings (no problem there), the network deciding when enough is enough (though Dan mentions they'll film at least 70 episodes), how long the cast wants to continue, and how long Dan wants to continue. But so far, Dan and the *iCarly* crew show no signs of slowing down, and with the show's tremendous success, Nick is still giving it its full support. Just ask Nick VP Marjorie Cohn, who publicly confirmed the network's faith in the show: "We just love

Jennette attending the 2009 Country Music Awards. Hopefully one day she won't just be attending the award ceremony, she'll be up on stage!

this show so much. We're going to continue to make it and hopefully it will continue to be incredibly well received." And the network's prez has given it her full support as well: Cyma Zharghami told the *LA Times*, "Nothing would make me happier than to watch *iCarly* have a really long life cycle."

Even when they're on hiatus from *iCarly*'s hectic filming schedule, the cast keeps busy on other projects. Miranda took some time to do voice-over work for the new 3-D animated film *Despicable Me*, which stars Steve Carell as Gru, the world's number two supervillain, who is plotting to steal the moon. But his evil schemes are interrupted by three orphan girls (one played by Miranda) who want to make Gru into their diabolical daddy (though it seems like Gru is so bad he would make Sam's mom look like a perfect parent). *The Lost Stallion*, a movie Miranda made way back before *iCarly*, was finally released on DVD in October 2009. Miranda plays Hannah Mills, a girl who photographs wild horses and learns about what threatens their survival.

Miranda's also been tapped for a proposed Paramount and Nickelodeon film called *How Could You Do This to Me?*, which reverses the traditional *Parent Trap* plot: in this case Miranda's character would be trying to prevent her divorced parents from getting back together!

In 2009, Jennette can be seen in *Minor Details*, a teen mystery about four friends trying to get to the bottom of a rash of sickness at Danforth High. Jennette plays Mia, one of the prime suspects! The film was released straight to DVD on February 5. For more *iCarly* cast goodness, watch for Jennette in *True Jackson, VP*, and Nathan in *CSI*.

Nickelodeon's making the most of their talented *iCarly* cast, and Jennette and Jerry continue their onscreen hilarity in the Nick original movie *Best Player*. Jerry plays Quincy, a video game master who, threatened with eviction from his parents' house, must win the prize money in a major tournament to keep up his lifestyle. The only thing that stands in his way? The current multi-player champion, "Prodigy" (played by Jennette). Network exec Marjorie Cohn called it "a funny and compelling story about online gaming taken to the extreme" and noted that the flick "gives Jerry Trainor and Jennette McCurdy a new platform in which to showcase their talent." Filmed in Vancouver, Canada, Jennette's frequent tweets from the *Best Player* set are both enthusiastic ("great day on set. jerry had me cracking up, janet is so cool, and i scared amir very badly") and tantalizing ("If I told you what the cast of 'the best player' had to do on set today, you wouldn't believe me...").

It's been a wild ride so far, filled with big laughs, bacon, ointment, and Penny Tees. Though even Spencer's Magic Meatball can't predict what's in store for *iCarly*, viewers know that whether it's playing the trumpet on a pogo stick or acting in a hit TV show, star power speaks for itself. So keep tuning in, people of Earth.

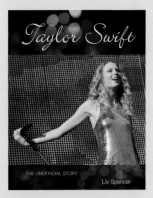

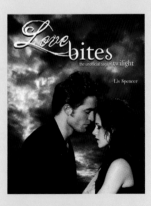
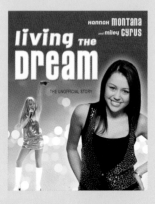